DO WE EXPECT MORE
OF MARRIAGE
THAN ANY OTHER KIND OF
RELATIONSHIP?

Today, men and women approach marriage with more doubts and greater expectations than ever before. The modern couple wants equality, seeks to preserve individuality, anticipates better sex, and yearns for a new belief in old values.

In her fascinating new book, Nena O'Neill explains how starting with a realistic "marriage premise"—one that celebrates such time-honored ideals as giving and sharing—not only helps you cope better when problems arise but gives you the most basic and important key to marital success.

THE
MARRIAGE PREMISE

Nena O'Neill

THE MARRIAGE PREMISE
*A Bantam Book / published by arrangement with
M. Evans and Company, Inc.*

PRINTING HISTORY
Evans edition published October 1977
2nd printing .... November 1977
Bantam edition / November 1978

*In most cases the names of individuals mentioned or quoted in
the text have been changed.*
*The Jeff Greenfield quotations in Chapter 13 are from his
article, "What I Learned About Myself from My Three Year
Old Daughter," which appeared in* GLAMOUR, *September 1976.
Copyright © 1976 by Jeff Greenfield. Reprinted by permission
of The Sterling Lord Agency, Inc.*
*The Robert Seidenberg quotations in Chapter 15 are from
his book,* Marriage in Life and Literature. *Copyright © 1970
by Robert Seidenberg. Reprinted by permission of Philosophical
Library.*

ISBN 0–553–11830–7

Published simultaneously in the United States and Canada

To Agnes, Leo, Michael, Brian
and, most of all, George

Preface

During all of the enormous changes of the last few decades, the durability of marriage, love, and commitment has come into question. Part of the loss of heart, the disillusionment, and the uncertainty about the institution of marriage has been unavoidable. The demands of change and the unsettling transformations we must make in any crisis force us to reexamine our assumptions and premises about life, ourselves, the world around us, our relationships, our marriages. But change does not necessarily mean loss as much as it does a reordering of our priorities. And crisis means a recombination of the old and the new into unfamiliar patterns that offer us opportunity and challenge. Now that we have come through the transition, what we have ended up with is a more realistic view of marriage. In the process of shedding some ideas and myths we have found that some time-honored premises are more valuable than ever before.

This book has been, for me, a reexamination and reaffirmation of certain constants in marriage. It is a personal book, and I have used many of my personal experiences, where they seemed relevant, to illustrate my point of view. It is also a departure, this time, from my continuing collaboration in research and writing with my husband, George.

Five years ago, when George and I wrote our first book, we were reflecting the desires and hopes of men and women caught in the midst of changing expectations. Marriage could no longer be lived in just one way. *Open Marriage* was and is our vision of what marriage can ideally be in a world of change: two people sharing their inner selves on a journey of change and growth, in a relationship of equality where each partner's individuality contributes to and augments the unity they share. It was and is our belief that marriage in the future would endure only through a strong emotional bond, through genuine caring for each other and an adaptability to change. In *Shifting Gears* we explored how individuals could meet personal change and crisis and become more self-supportive and giving in their relationships with others. Since then, marriage has indeed changed and is now lived in a diversity of styles and designs.

This book represents my search for the common ground we all share in marriage, no matter what kind we have. Whether it is a traditional marriage, an open marriage, or one that is somewhere in between, whether it is my marriage, my parents' marriage, or yours, there are certain constants that have not changed. These are the basic premises underlying all marriages.

For me, this book has been a journey of discovery, a collaboration with the events and people that have had meaning in my life and with the many people who have been involved in its creation. My deepest thanks to my husband, George O'Neill, whose under-standing, insights, contributions, endurance, criticism, and devotion I respect and appreciate more than ever before. That we remain best friends and still married through the pressures that the writing of this book has caused in our domestic life is no miracle but a tribute, either to that enduring solidarity I make so much of in this book, or to our very seasoned love for each other. It is probably both.

I am deeply grateful to all those who have assisted me not only with their time, expertise, or special con-tributions, but with their caring: to my publisher, Herb Katz, for precipitating this journey and for his many hours of consultation; to my editor, Joyce Christmas, for her indefatigable and cheerful per-sistence and selectiveness; to Nina Beckwith, Haskell Hoffenberg, Nancy Abel, Esther Shefrin, David Shefrin, Pam Veley, and Lynn Schwartz; to Frances Kamm for her endless hours of transcription and to all those who pitched in to help at one time or another.

To those couples and individuals I talked with, whose thoughts and feelings form a substantial part of this book, I owe a special debt of gratitude. They are the ones who are living out their marriages through the inconsistencies of our times, in conflict and devotion, in love and compassion, in hope and belief. It is my hope that this book will reaffirm for many others those values we have always cherished in human relationships. Marriage still remains that unique relationship which offers us the profound sat-isfactions and rewards of experiences shared with another in love, commitment, and the excitement that makes a life a true adventure.

Nena O'Neill

Contents

What greater thing is there for two human souls than to feel that they are joined for life, to strengthen each other in all labor, to rest on each other in all sorrow, to minister to each other in all pain, to be one with each other in silent unspeakable memories at the moment of last parting?

George Eliot

1

Beginnings

I remember my wedding day vividly. It was during wartime, George was in the service, and we were married over a weekend in a small church in a strange city, our parents traveling to be with us, arriving tired but elated, and there was all the excitement of taking this step, being very much in love—everything intensified by the immediacy of war.

We had met and fallen in love as students at Columbia University. Then our courtship became a hectic mix of long phone calls between classes and long trips on sooty, crowded trains to spend a few hours together. The war, with its separations and risks, was a fact of life to be dealt with, but beyond were the dreams and ideals and adventures we wanted to live together. We have lived them, for thirty-three years. We have changed them; they have changed us.

When we married we had no doubt that we would have children and become a family. We accepted, out of faith and tradition, certain premises about marriage and family. We would become three or more, four as it turned out. I would be nurturer, healer, comforter, hearth keeper, the shelter in the storm for my husband and children. George would be provider, protector, the head of the family. Though we had some ideals that were different from those of most young marrieds, we didn't question the principal roles of husband and wife, mother and father.

We also had the images of love and high romance that came to everyone through the orchestrated bliss of thirties and forties movies—Ginger Rogers and Fred Astaire dancing around the world, Dorothy McGuire and Robert Young in *The Enchanted Cottage,* and Marie and Pierre Curie making history in their lab, and especially Myrna Loy and William Powell as Nick and Nora in *The Thin Man,* who were, to the girl from the Midwest I was then, the utmost in married sophistication. No grand passion, but they were witty, smooth, and having a lot of fun.

Those images were important to me, and so, too, was the togetherness theme of the fifties as we shifted into second gear in our marriage. We did realize some of our dreams, we did find the adventures we sought, we did go to exotic places, and through it all we had our children with us. It was a lot of fun, and there was also a lot of rough going as well. All the dreams had to be reconciled with the reality of making ends meet, a baby slung over my hip as I climbed through Mexican ruins and sorted potsherds while trying to stop our four-year-old from wandering into the jungle; the moments of discouragement had to be accepted along with the magic and the thrills.

For all our tough times and limitations, we of the forties and fifties may have had it easier than people starting out today. Our options were restricted, our expectations assimilated. Betty Friedan to the contrary (welcome prophet though she was), all my years of being my husband's cheerleader, chief cook and bottle washer, and partner in research were not all that bad. A lot has changed; most of us then were too busy just surviving—having children, sewing snowsuits, fixing cast-off furniture, finding apartments and the money to pay dentists' bills, and getting an education—to worry about something called personal growth. At least we certainly didn't sit and talk about it in those terms. We were facing up to life, and we didn't like a lot of it. But we were also growing with each responsibility assumed and each decision made.

Under the pressures of the new liberations, new ideas of growth, greater expectations, and changing roles, I have had to look again at my own marriage and those of others. The very foundations of marriage appear to have shifted beneath our feet, as though an earthquake had toppled the temples and altered the face of the city. The revolutions of the last few decades have brought change and questioning in all areas.

If my marriage had not had a solid base, a long history of shared experiences and responsibilities along with the joys and adventures, if we had not known each other down to the roots of our beings, the changes in concepts and ideals over the last decades might have rocked our marriage more than they did.

I know these times of change have been confusing. But among all the changes and paradoxes and confusions, marriage continues to bring me satisfaction and rewards well worth the compromise and struggle.

Marriage is a crucible—whether it ends after six years like my son's, is still alive after thirty-three years like mine, or lasts a lifetime like my parents'—

and in it we are constantly distilling ourselves and our experiences in life. Our deepest emotions, our most primitive needs, our deficiencies and our strengths are all subjected to the heat of that crucible. We are changed by it—for better or worse. The fictions we have created, the preconceptions we started with, the images, are ever-present and interwoven with the realities we live, in our personalities, our past and present and perceived future.

For all the books and preaching and counseling and psychological knowledge we have today, for all our new ideals of freedom and our emphasis on personal growth and fulfillment, marriage is still basically two people trying to love each other and answer each other's needs. It may not be forever, it may have changed, but it still gives us opportunities no other relationship can give us. And whether or not any specific marriage lasts forever is really irrelevant to the value of marriage itself. It has its own special character and value and offers its own special opportunities, which I have tried to examine here in a new perspective.

Marriage may not be the answer for everyone, or for a whole lifetime—that is our option today. But if we do choose marriage, let us know what we choose it for, why it is valuable, and how precious even in its imperfections it can become in every present moment.

2

Change

For each of us there is an event, a deeply emotional experience, that sets off a storm of questioning. We come through it changed, with new insights and a reassessment of our values. The breakup of my son's marriage was such an event, not only for him but for me as well.

It may be I was even more disrupted by my son's divorce than I would otherwise have been, had I not spent the last ten years of my life thinking, studying, and writing about marriage. While my husband and I were working on *Open Marriage* and *Shifting Gears*, and during the time after those books were published, we talked to hundreds of people all over the United

States and abroad. Hundreds more wrote to us frankly about their experiences and their problems. Marriage in a period of radical change became the central concern of our professional lives, and we as a couple came to symbolize many of the contemporary views of marriage. Perhaps I did not realize how very deep that concern was until it hit me where I live.

The day my son's marriage was over I felt abandoned and resentful. Most of all, the aching hurt of his suffering cut through me. I knew he was not blameless, that he and his wife were trying to work out their own destinies. I know that nothing is simple in marriage; no breakup is a clear cause-and-effect situation. There are currents of reason and emotion and X-factors we can never untangle. In my helplessness to comfort my son and heal his sorrow, I felt paralyzed, confused, defeated, full of guilt. Michael's problems and his anguish forced me to look at everything in my own life—my relationship with my husband, with our younger son, with my parents, with myself.

I remembered so many things that had happened, the events and the problems, the good times and the perplexing ones we all went through during his childhood, the things we would like to change if we could do it all over again, and all the mistakes we as parents think we have made. Could we have been more than we were then?

I remembered things like the birthday present he gave me when he was an eager twelve-year-old. It was a set of steak knives he had carefully selected and bought with money he earned delivering groceries. I said they were lovely and thanked him, and then scolded him for spending his money on something we could have done without, gave him a penny for the knives, as one does superstitiously for these presents. But no mountain of pennies could bury the pain I feel every time I think of how little it would have taken not to scold, to make him feel proud of his choice, to make him feel loved for it. But I was too involved in my own ideas of right and wrong, duty and thrift. Still, I was as affectionate and fully loving as I could be.

I tried to give my sons a sense of integrity about life and people, to give them a sense of honor, and they have rewarded, gratified, and delighted me through the years. And yet, with Michael's divorce, I felt I had failed him. Even knowing that divorce is not a failure and knowing that they would grow to be better persons through it didn't make it any easier.

I had thought Michael and Anne would be together forever. Not that anything lasts forever these days, but they had so much going for them. They were so much in love, so tender and caring toward each other. He is a fine young man, sensitive, talented, strong, ambitious. She is a fine young woman, gifted, without artifice, and beautiful with a clarity of features and heart that is striking. We wondered, as her parents did, why they wanted to get married so soon, so young. But who was to fault them for making the commitment? We, too, had married young. I cried at the wedding, my hand locked in my husband's, and laughed with the bride's mother as we wiped away each other's tears—two sentimental women with bright hopes for their children, aware of the long road ahead.

When it broke apart I felt it couldn't be happening, not to my son, not to me. I had always believed that if you wanted to make anything work, it would work. Besides, there had never been a divorce in either George's or my family. Yes, a stray aunt or uncle here and there whose wild fling ended in a welcome return to hearth and home, some separations, but mostly a long line of solid, staid marriages, lasting till death did them part.

Michael had never been one to lean on others. He had struck out on his own, getting jobs as a kid, discovering his own skills and interests, going on a riteof-passage adventure in Mexico, making his career a huge success by his own efforts. He had always been independent, and yet he seemed very dependent in his devotion to Anne. There was love all over the place, seeping out of the cracks in the walls, flowing out of their hearts in a way that was almost unbearably endearing.

Early in their marriage, Michael and Anne talked to us openly about their hopes and joys, their problems in adjustment, about managing their life together, about their friends, their careers. As they began to grapple more seriously with their problems, they drifted away from us. At first it seemed the natural separation of young marrieds into their own lives. Then, after a while, I knew something was wrong. You always know, in a thousand small ways. But this wasn't something I could fix or make right again for Michael, as I had once held him close when he cried as a child. Nor could I tell him what I had learned in all my years of marriage, which might have helped. Parents shouldn't interfere, should they? I knew that rough spots iron out; they had for us, for others. But Michael and Anne no longer asked for advice or talked about themselves with us.

How could we know what was best for him, for her? Could I have loved him more, made him stronger, so that it didn't seem the end of the world when they began to hurt each other? Where had we failed? George and I had the ordinary grab bag everyone is handed in life—the good and the bad, the rough and the beautiful. If our marriage had been smoother, would his have been better? So I ran the film of my life, our family's past, questioning and wondering.

Then it was enough. The time comes to balance the score, to recognize the strengths and see the thread of goodness and devotion running through our lives. I realized that Michael had to grow emotionally on his own, just as I had to by tackling my guilt, by trying to see things rationally rather than through tilted emotions. Most of us want to grow more than inches beyond our parents and our backgrounds: That growth can spell a lot of good and dispel a lot of hell. Most of us hope that our marriages will be more than just a little more understanding, less demanding, and more loving than our parents'.

In the trauma of separating from his wife, Michael was also fighting his own inner battle. In a painful divorce a person tends to feel all alone, as if reliving a primeval abandonment. As a parent I too felt abandoned, rejected, shut out in the cold. Whether or not we wish to interfere in our children's lives, we are there in habits and attitudes, in concepts of good and bad, as reminders of where they came from and perhaps how far they have to go.

In accepting each other, Michael and Anne had also accepted the parents who had nurtured and formed them, and their marriage had joined our two families in the fabric of kinship. When it split apart we were all torn and left with frazzled edges of emptiness. Our lives had been enriched by becoming in-laws, our bonds had multiplied, our holidays had been more festive because we had planned and spent them together. Try as we may to enliven them, holidays are now big gaps, missing the glow, the feeling of family connection we all once shared.

Too often it is only in the loss of something that we learn its value and importance in our lives. When Michael married and I knew he was loved and cared for and that he returned that love, my own security increased. When his marriage broke apart I reacted with all the pain and protectiveness, guilt and anger of any mother, despite my years of study and, I thought, professional objectivity. But it made me think more deeply about the value of marriage. I realized that my feeling of loss came not only from his sorrow but from the loss of order in his life, and of the protection and connectedness that marriage embodies. I felt more keenly the sense of place in marriage, the enveloping warmth it can bring, the anchor it can provide. Where else can we feel so safe, not being out there alone with the world's winds blowing at our unprotected backs?

Another young man, recently divorced, wrote to us from California, describing this very feeling. On his way home from a Parents Without Partners meeting he saw a middle-aged couple on a lighted porch "just sitting, not talking it seemed, just sitting and watching the people and the cars go by and feeling the warm night breezes flow against them. I stopped the car and somehow felt this was where I wanted to be. Why is it, I thought, why is this so hard to get, nothing more, just this? . . . What keeps all of us who are divorced from being able to enjoy this peaceful scene, this simple calm? . . . Isn't this an easy place to go if you really want to?"

No, it isn't an easy place to get to, and all the good intentions, all the admirable objectives, all the greater awareness of our individual needs, all this doesn't make it any easier. It may even make it harder. My son and daughter-in-law had all the essentials for a good contemporary marriage, growing up as they had in a more open climate with greater psychological awareness, greater affluence, more information than my generation. Their premises for themselves and for their marriage incorporated many of the new ideals—belief in equality, respecting each other's individuality and right to grow in his or her own career. All these are aspects of my own concept of marriage, and worthy, in many cases essential, attitudes to bring to marriage today.

But isn't marriage also more burdened today than ever before? My son and his wife were struggling not only with all the new concepts of equality in roles and opportunity for personal growth, but with all the tried and true basics of marriage—belonging, having a home base and a network of family, recognizing limits and obligations. Marriages today are part of a society that is no longer stable, but shifting constantly. The gentle rate of evolution of past decades has been accelerated—what is here today may be gone, or at least different, tomorrow. We have had to adapt to changes that our parents never dreamed of. We are in a time of transition, having to assimilate the genuine new gains with the legacy of the past. We are rejecting spurious advancements of the recent revolutions, the things that don't seem to work after all, while we sift through to find the things that really do matter. It is not an easy task.

We have just come through a period of unprecedented focus on the self and the search for *me*, what *I* am, what *I* want, what *my* future is, what *my* needs are. It has taken its toll on marriage. We have downgraded the "us" in marriage because we were so dedicated to the search for the "me." In the turmoil of the sixties, many people ignored the sharing aspects of marriage because they were trying so hard to break out of the total-togetherness syndrome. In our haste to correct the obvious inadequacies of the old order in marriage, to revise our roles, and to eradicate the traditions we saw as confining, once again the baby has been thrown out with the bathwater.

It seems to me that marriages today are turning back, not to the old closed coercions and external pressures, but to new combinations and a reappraisal of what marriage can still offer. Freedom, the catchword of the sixties, has a new meaning in our lives today. We are not, after all, absolutely free; no one is entitled to "give" us freedom. What we are entitled to is the knowledge that no one may take our freedom away, that in marriage we freely choose to become husband and wife, to accept the necessary compromises of marriage which may mean less freedom in some areas, more in others, to be interdependent in a context where our individuality is fully accepted.

Marriage is also once again being prized for its

response to another great cry of our times—security. As the old order gives way to the new, we are coming to realize that many of the old foundations of marriage are still firm, and that we can still build on them.

3

Marriage Makes a Family

Whether it is a _Lohengrin_-and-champagne production number, a City Hall quickie, or barefoot in the park with folk rock and frozen yogurt, the wedding is where it begins. The simplest ceremony marks marriage as a special relationship.

Ginny and Hal had been living together for four years and then decided on the spur of the moment to get married. For all their beliefs in open and free relationships, when they made the public commitment something happened.

Ginny: Somehow I never anticipated that this little ceremony was actually going to mean anything.

You see it on television and you see your parents'
dressed-up pictures, and we went through it in
the most mundane manner.

Hal: We had always pictured just running off to a
Justice of the Peace or someone. We'd lived together for those four years, and suddenly Ginny
told me she had the rings. I didn't think it was
going to be particularly enjoyable, but I really
felt romantic getting married.

Ginny: There were only the magistrate and two jani-
tors as witnesses, and yet when he said, "Do you
forever . . ." or whatever the words are, I felt like
crying. I almost didn't get the words out. It was
touching in a way I didn't anticipate.

Hal: There we were, holding hands behind our backs,
giving secret little hand signals, to show we already knew what he was telling us. We had already had that bond for a long time.

Ginny: Yes, but he symbolized in those few words of
the ceremony what we'd already decided on. He
verbalized it in a simple and succinct way.

What was being achieved in this simple ceremony
was a great deal more than getting two signatures on
a piece of paper. "It was establishing the one special
thing we could do for each other," said Hal. "We
knew we would intermingle with other people, but
whatever might happen in the future, this was one
thing I could still give Ginny, this reassurance, this
commitment." Ginny added that she feels "more solid
by the fact that I'm married. I've made a commitment
and I know what I'm talking about in the relationship."

Not only does the ceremony have the force of tradition behind it and the weight of history contained
in its words, it is also our personal acknowledgment
that we are passing into a different state in life.

At the other end of the ceremonial spectrum was
Connie's wedding. It was a splendid affair, with long
dresses and candles, flowers and champagne, a won-

derful party that some ten years later guests still recall as a memorable occasion. With two babies now and her doctor husband in the midst of a grueling residency, Connie recalls that "when we talked about getting married, I didn't care what I wore, but it was important to Paul to do it right. My father's the same way. I guess men don't have to deal with the nitty-gritty of living the way women do, so they can be more romantic.

"I also didn't care how I got married or where. Now I think that's a wrong idea, and I'm glad we did have a big wedding. I think a ceremony that takes a while is better than a you-want-to-get-married?-OK,-you're-married thing, which is like getting a driver's license. You need something to impress on you that you've changed the rules now, you can't get out of it. You've said, 'That's it, I have to make it work.' You need something to show you that something big has really happened, and it's happened to lots of people, and there are familiar words to cover the situation."

Something does happen to each of us and to us together when we marry. This "something" immediately changes our destiny, the way we look at each other, and the way the world looks at us.

Judy, a bright, vivacious young woman who works for a textbook publisher, got married a year and a half ago, after "living back and forth between our two apartments for a couple of years." Talking about the actual ceremony, she said, "We did it legally and publicly and in front of people, and it really meant something, the public statement of being married. I hate to admit it, but I was so insecure that the ring on my finger made me much calmer in terms of us and going home and even doing separate things."

When we marry, we step across the threshold into a new home—often literally into a new house, and certainly into a new status. It is not by chance that the traditional Jewish marriage ceremony takes place under a canopy, called a chuppa, or that the Russians

had a house of marriage, or that in Guatemala a long
string of filigree beads, such as the beautiful set I
have, is placed around the heads of both bride and
groom to symbolize their new position in life. In some
primitive cultures the young couple enters a special
new hut to consummate their marriage.

With all the changes in our society today, I think
we have forgotten the importance of those symbols
and of what they stand for. These images of home
and family are entwined by custom into the rituals of
the marriage ceremony. The rites may be a holdover
from the time when marriage was seen mainly in procreative terms, but their value can be reinterpreted
today in the light of our understanding that the couple itself constitutes a family, consciously choosing in
marriage the security and traditions of family life.
The ceremony celebrates a new creation, for ourselves
and for society. We join our beings, our backgrounds
and our futures, together into a new entity which
deserves to be recognized as a family, whether or not
there are children.

Elaine, who has been married nearly two years, is
a modern young woman with a demanding career
who grew up in the changes of the sixties. She told
me, "We were committed to each other when we
were living together, but something different happens when you're married. I feel he's my family. My
parents are my family, but when I think of my immediate family now, I think of Ken. Before we were
married, there was a definite sense of 'his family' and
'my family.' I had always seen myself as my mother
and father's daughter, and suddenly I had the sense
that we, Ken and I, were building our own family,
and I was his best friend and wife, in the nicest sense
of the word."

It is easy to recognize the inherent nature of marriage as creating a family when there are children,
the concrete evidence of our being together both
physically and spiritually. It isn't so easy to recognize

marriage as a family unit when there are no children. Today, even though more and more couples choose not to have children at all, some people still tend to regard the marriage without children as a frivolous venture. We often fail to recognize the character of marriage in and of itself as a special commitment and form of order in life.

Such a sense of commitment was expressed by a handsome, fortyish man who had recently remarried: "We *are* a family, just the two of us. We didn't want to just live together; we chose to marry and we think of ourselves alone as a family. So I resent it when others treat us like singles off on a lark. We chose not to have children, but that doesn't make our commitment any the less strong or meaningful. We know what we mean to each other."

The strong sense that their marriage alone creates a family is also felt by couples who plan to have children in the future. Their relationship is not in limbo until then; the years alone together can strengthen their marriage and build for their future.

Tim and Mary recently celebrated their fourth wedding anniversary. Both come from working-class Boston backgrounds, and met while attending college. Mary continued on to get a master's degree in education at night while teaching school in the day, and Tim is beginning to make a success of his small advertising agency.

"I'd like to have three or four kids," Tim said, "and my wife would too, but we'd be out of our minds if we had one now, before I've established myself in business. Mary and I can't see making our lives miserable financially just to have a kid. I've only been married four years, and that's four years I've had with my wife, the two of us alone, and we'll never have that again, ever, once we have children. We've gotten to know each other and we've got a good, solid relationship now. A kid is going to take a little bit away from that, but I'm willing to sacrifice that.

"But even if we never have children, we do have something. Marriage gives you a family—my wife is really my only family. Last Thanksgiving we went to my parents' house. My mother was there, my father, my brother, and my sister and her husband and their two kids. It was a nice day, a family day, but it was different from when I was a kid. It was my family, sure, but it's a secondary family. My family is my wife and myself. I was very content to go home, because that's where I belong."

Marisa and Jon worked for eight years before they had children, Jon as a salesman and Marisa as a secretary. Now that they have two small daughters, Marisa says, "We're both surprised that children really add something to a marriage, not subtract. I don't know why we thought it was going to be different, but it never occurred to us that it would be so important. Jon always assumed that we'd have kids, that was one of his reasons for marrying me, but I had always seen it as an option—until I had a six-month-old baby. Then it occurred to me that children really are terribly important. It's the best thing we ever did. We could have done it earlier as well, but I wouldn't have known that."

Now that children are no longer necessarily a part of it, how does contemporary marriage stack up against the classic definitions?

Most traditional definitions of marriage include the sharing of a residence, reciprocal economic and sexual obligations of husband and wife, the obligations of parenthood, a division of labor, a unit of primary relationships, tying into a network of other families through kinship. And contemporary marriages do, by and large, contain most of those elements, except for a few interesting changes reflecting the social and economic changes of recent years. For instance, even though husbands and wives of today may be reversing their traditional roles, or sharing and exchanging tasks, they are still dividing the work for better efficiency. And many of the dual-career couples are living apart, in long-distance or part-time marriages, not even sharing a residence on a full-time basis. But the greatest change has been in the economic basis for marriage. With more and more women working today, marriage partners are less economically dependent and more economically interdependent.

Living Together

For various financial, legal, and personal reasons, more and more people today, and people of all kinds —the young, the old, college students, never marrieds, and the divorced—are choosing to live together instead on marrying. They want to experiment, they are not sure of the future, they have been in bad marriages before, or they have seen too many others go through the pain and hassles of separation and divorce. They are frankly afraid and wonder if the commitment to marriage is worth it.

Elaine, whose husband had been married previously, remarked, "People say things very cavalierly when they're afraid. We were asked what music we wanted at our wedding, and Ken said, 'Maybe This Time.' I wondered if maybe he didn't wonder and have doubts. He had said he didn't worry about his previous one, but maybe he did have doubts, even though this time it was a thirty-three-year-old man who was making a real choice to get married. There were still times when he said, 'Can we do this? We're so happy now, living together. Why get married?' "

Besides the fear we have of legal bonds there are many reasons to choose living together rather than marriage. Diane, who has two children, sees "no use for a contract in a relationship without children. The only meaning a contract has is to protect the children, and that is something I take very seriously. Marriage is a very serious commitment to family."

Many people agree with Diane. Why get married

at all, unless you intend to have children? Aren't children the raison d'être of marriage? Well, we've seen that a lot of people don't feel that way; they marry whether children are in their future or not. I believe that many of us want and need the structure and benefits of marriage, with or without children, however we choose to live it.

It is undeniable, however, that these days the distinction between living together and marriage often becomes blurred, its edges running in and out of each other like the patterns in watered-silk taffeta. Some of the confusion comes from parents who try hard to believe that their chilren's living-together arrangements are like a marriage. Living-togethers do look a lot like marrieds. We see them creating a home, buying furniture, having sexual fidelity, even having children. These are couples who have a very strong commitment in their relationship. In less liberal days they were considered scandalous; in the present day, they are far more accepted.

Sally and Stan have lived together for more than seven years, ever since their college days. It began as a casual arrangement, but over the years they have grown more and more committed to each other, until they are almost indistinguishable from all the young married couples who live in the small Connecticut town where they recently bought a house. Sally says of their relationship, "Initially when I started living with Stan, I thought I was making some kind of statement, that I wouldn't accept certain values that society has, but I don't feel that way anymore. I don't look down on anybody who gets married or who is married, but I don't see any reason for it. I look at myself as being married, except that it isn't legal.

"My parents have accepted it, but it's taken time. Now I can go home to their house and sleep in the same bed with Stan. The last time I was home, my mother said, 'It's just like he's a son-in-law.' Yet my parents would like us to be married for appearance's sake, but they realize that for all intents and purposes, I am married. Well, I am."

Couples like Sally and Stan don't seem to need the support of the ceremony. For them, and couples like them, living together is a satisfying and fulfilling way of being together. It affords them a freedom of movement and a kind of development no other relationship gives them. For some, living together may be a constructive step toward marriage, a time to experiment, to learn, to test, a transition from singlehood to marriage. Or it can be, as it is for Sally and Stan, a permanent life-style, valid in its own right. But long-term living-together couples are aware that there is a difference between living together and marriage, even though they boast that their relationship is the same as or even better than marriage. They feel somehow that if they marry things will be different.

"Will marriage change me?" asked Mimi, pondering the possibility of marriage with the young man she had been living with for four years. "I really don't know. I want to get married, but life is so good now. If you want to know the truth, what I keep worrying about is, will marriage change me? Will it change him? What we have now is just right for us and I don't want it to change." Mimi's instincts are right. Marriage *does* change us. Just as any close relationship changes us and transforms us as individuals.

Polly, who has been living with Mark for nearly eight years, hesitates when it comes to marriage for fear that it will bring a kind of finality, a static resolution to the relationship. "We were going to get married last fall," she told me, "but we didn't. We felt we had things to work out before we could actually make a final commitment. I particularly was worried that if we actually finalized our relationship, we would no longer continue to work out the things we had been working out. The question I asked myself was, 'Would you want to spend the rest of your life with Mark as it is right now? Period. No change. Absolutely the way it is right now, forever and ever, Amen.' And I said, no, I didn't."

Actually, Polly's and Mimi's fears are one and the same. They represent a legitimate wariness toward the institution and the ways in which marriage *could* make their relationship rigid.

Unlike Sally and Stan, who do have a strong commitment in their relationship, there are, of course, many people who have a living-together arrangement for fun, as an experiment, a temporary situation. These are among the options offered to us by today's more liberal sexual climate, and should in no way be confused with marriage. Living together in this way may suit the people involved very well, give them romance, bliss, and the degree of togetherness they need, but marriage it is not, and those are not the subjects of our discussion here.

Connie pointed out the difference she sees between marriage and a living-together arrangement: "Everybody fights from time to time, and somebody has to apologize first and make it all well. When you're married as opposed to living together, you don't have the luxury of slamming out and saying, 'Well, I'm moving out,' because you know you're going to have to fix it up tomorrow morning. So you might as well stop in the middle of the argument and fix it up now, before you get too far in."

Charlie spoke about the difference from the point of view of a man who has been married nearly twenty years: "You have the expectation that there's going to be a future when you're married. There's always a sense of planning, the sense that the two of you are going to do something X number of years from now, the idea that you have made some sort of vow you're going to make good on. It gives you a kind of structure; it colors every activity in the present in terms of what's going to happen later. For people living together, drama and conflict may result from reluctance to discuss the future. Often when there's talk about the future, they're very shy about it: Will there be a Christmas? What will we be doing next year at vacation time? In marriage your life is structured. There's a sort of comfort there, there's a sense of ordering. People take vows to get themselves into a pattern where they know who they are when they wake up in the morning."

Marriage, then, implies the building of a future together. It is a commitment to the promise that you *do* have a future together. By contrast, the future in most living-together arrangements is decidedly open-ended—at some point the arrangement will end, either in separation or in marriage. And if the going gets rough, there is always an out.

Jeannie, who has been married to Ray for twelve years, recalls how the formal bond of marriage helped them to weather serious difficulties in the early years of their marriage and to arrive at their present happy, mature, and solid relationship. "Marriage is an institution, and if it weren't for the institution, I'd be alone right now. It held us together in the first seven years when we would have drifted apart. It was like some kind of glue that kept us fixed in each other's affairs, even when Ray started spending a lot of nights out until four A.M. His mind was someplace else, not on the marriage, and he was hassling out a lot of problems. I remember thinking that if we were not married, he would not have come home at all. If it weren't for marriage, it would have been just another relationship ended.

"The glue, the institution, holds together as many unhappy marriages as happy ones. There's just some kind of bond, and for us, it gave us time to work things out."

A View of Our Own

Bronislaw Malinowski, the anthropologist, referred to the "almost mystical bond" between husband and wife that exists in most human societies. Religions have compared it to the transcendent oneness we seek with the divine. I do believe these mystical bonds exist and that the oneness is experienced in a spiritual way. Love and caring help create the human bonds we feel.

We see the initial tug between newly marrieds as they develop their unity in practical matters. They have to agree on a life-style, where they are going to live, how much time they will spend together, what they will buy, who their friends will be, who will do what in the household. They must make innumerable decisions on what is important to them individually and as a couple, on what they feel might be harmful to them and their union. There is a social as well as a private identity now to be considered.

Marriage partners educate each other and smooth the rough edges of each other's behavior. They become mirrors for their partner, reflecting the other's private and public actions. They share with each other their knowledge, backgrounds, and experiences, likes and dislikes.

"Jim expects me to try things," Pauline said. "Things I never conceived of or wanted to do. You don't have to like it or continue doing it, but you have to make a full effort. Now he wants to try hang gliding and I draw the line there. I could go and watch him hurt himself, but I won't do it. But that doesn't mean I'm saying to him that he can't go hang gliding. Otherwise that's sort of like saying that your wedding day is the end of so much of yourself; you're sort of betraying yourself. And I expect him to try things, too, I want to give him something he never had before. He never used to go to the theater, and I grew up going to shows with my parents. I love it. I got him into Off-Broadway stuff, and he'd never done that before. Now I think he would go on his own, even if I couldn't go; he really loves it."

Through time and the myriad events shared, the

couple develops its own habits, traditions, and rituals. All the practical matters and emotional issues they work out as a couple combine to form a psychological set that becomes uniquely their own. They decide on their common and individual goals and discover their common purpose. Yet each still remains a separate person, contributing personal qualities and opinions and even disagreements to the entity that is their relationship, each drawing from it new perspectives about himself or herself.

The couple welds together their backgrounds to form a common frame of reference, similar to the way families—mother, father, brothers and sisters—regard themselves as a unit and often develop a common perspective in the way they look out on the world. It is not a tartan alone that distinguishes a MacGregor from a MacTavish, but his special point of view and behavior toward the world as well. The couple may develop a special perspective quite different from that of either of their parental families, or they may, like Diane and Stephen, be comfortable with a viewpoint consciously grounded in their own backgrounds.

Diane: I'm not sure my marriage is all that different from my parents' marriage, and I think the continuity in our situation is probably greater than it is in many a modern household, where there seems to be so much of a departure.

Stephen: Diane's family and my family had known each other for a long time. In fact, there are parts of her family that I probably know better than she does. And it's not so much that I know hers and she knows mine as that we come from enough of a similar background that our reactions and attitudes are reflective of that background.

Diane: We were both married before, and the first time around, I had selected a very artistic, intellectual person, and I got very involved in a sort of avant-garde life-style which was not terribly to my liking. When I went into this marriage, it was very much a question of having realized that here was someone very familiar to me, and at that point in my life, it felt right. Even though we still have our disagreements from time to time, this is a relationship that I know I should be involved in, and I can stop worrying about that and worry about the form and shape of my own life and how I want to live it.

We can recognize the identity of married couples in many ways, tangible and intangible. We notice the "couple aura" that surrounds them; they do look different and act differently when they are together. We sense the special private unity of newly married couples. Nancy is an example. "We went to a bar mitzvah last weekend for a friend's son, and a woman came up to us after the ceremony and asked, 'Are you newlyweds?' I said, 'Yes, thirty-five weeks ago tomorrow.' Then I asked her how she knew and she said, 'There's something going on between you that I just felt.'

"I guess it's true," Nancy added. "I know that my husband is my friend, and not just in the platonic sense. It's this total feeling also that we've got a secret. I have this feeling that nobody knows in the whole world what's really going on, what he and I giggle about and whisper about. What's really going on is sharing the way we look out on the world."

Love in marriage expands to become that "enduring, diffuse solidarity" anthropologist David Schneider has described in discussing kinship and marriage in America. Enduring, because there is a commitment to the future; diffuse, because it is not confined narrowly to a specific goal or a specific kind of behavior. Solidarity is built because the relationship is supportive, helpful, trusting, and cooperative.

The shared views, alignment of purpose, and unique ambience that married couples create becomes the "we" and "us" of marriage, a separate and distinct entity from the "me" and "you." Moreover, it is not a oneness that detracts from or deprives them of their individuality, but one they share and that transforms them, both as individuals and as a couple.

4

Golden Wedding

The last time we had been together at a family reunion, all of us together in one place at one time, was for my parents' golden wedding anniversary four years ago. We had piled into the house, shouting and hugging each other, with suitcases spilling over, the phone ringing, friends and aunts and uncles and cousins dropping in. There was laughter, tales of our children's exploits and troubles, the sharing of our own childhood memories.

My two brothers, their wives, George and I had planned and financed the event, the invitations, the ceremony, the food and the cake, musicians and the

hall. We reveled in the excitement, busying the tele-
phone lines between New York, Ohio, and Georgia,
happy to be able to present this celebration as our
gift to them, a gift for all those years they had given
us.

Fifty years together. Taken all together in a lump,
they boggled my mind, and yet they had piled up,
year after year, like thick snowflakes covering the
landscape, piling into drifts, soft mountains of love
and caring, some of them perhaps frozen by time and
habit.

Looking at their marriage, all those years of marriage, I saw my own thirty married years piling up,
flipping past like the pages in a book, some chapters
better than others, some sparkling with newness we
shared, some full of anguish and gloom, of gentle
closeness, some exciting or plodding or confused. Had
it been the same for them? What did all those years
together mean for them?

Years of commonplace things, of routine, of excitement over the events and crises of life. The miles of
scrubbed floors and tons of ironing, the endless days
my father left for work and came home in snow or
searing heat, the countless fall picnics and Sunday
dinners. The time the three of us children all had
chicken pox together. The time David broke his arm
riding his bike, and fourteen-year-old Jerry came
home from delivering newspapers drunk on cheap
wine. Our stomping, joyous parties. Their worry for
me, married to a young man during wartime, and for
David and Jerry when they went off to war. The
discipline, the trials they had with us, the songs my
mother sang to us, their encouragement to study and
to be fair and honest in our relationships, and take
the consequences of our own decisions, the times they
stood aside in the pain of letting go, and the small
treasures of moments of closeness.

"Today your friends, your family, and especially

we, your children, join in true celebration of the ties that support, nourish, and bind us together in spiritual oneness and human unity."

The solemnity of the occasion struck me most at the reception, as the hall quieted and we three children stood in front of the huge gathering while I read the short tribute I had written to our parents.

"We your children thank you for the gift of life, the guidance toward responsibility, and the model your life has been for caring for each other. The joy of your love and union has been the measure of our creation; the pain and sorrow, a measure of confirmation; and the constancy of your union, our reaffirmation.

"We, your family and friends, salute you for this past half century of life together and join you in joyous celebration and anticipation of the years to come."

I thanked them now for what I had once fought against, rebelled against—their way of life, which had seemed so solid and dependable that it was stultifying, so uneventful that it was boring, their adherence to their strict standards. And yet it was just that enduring solidarity they represented that had influenced me the most. Those two words, *enduring* and *solidarity,* made me see the many faces of love and commitment they implied. In those moments, I was seeing Mother and Dad mainly as parents, seeing them through the eyes of a grateful daughter who was close to fifty now, and who could now understand from experience what parenting and married love meant. It was just that dependability, that capacity for sticking it out that had carried me through many problems and crises.

But they were not only parents; they were also two people in a marriage of their own. I tried to picture them when they were first married, standing at the altar of that small church on the top of the mountain near their Pennsylvania farmhouse. They, too, had been starry-eyed young lovers, my father with pitch-black hair and a trim mustache, my mother slender and beautiful with auburn braids.

Fifty years behind them, and how many more to come? Earlier that morning, when they had restated their vows at Mass, I would have liked to hear church bells pealing loudly, see the aisles littered with flowers, decorations all over the church, with a festive, dressed-up crowd and the organ resounding across the hall and out through the windows. I half expected all that when I walked in, but St. Martha's, where I had knelt as a child, was quiet and unadorned. The church and the ceremony were as practical, straightforward, and unpretentious as their lives had been.

They stood there together at the altar, my mother a little stouter now, less sure of step, her auburn hair now short, wispy, covered with a soft wig. My father's shoulders were still squared, but his hair was thinning and gray. They held hands, one of his hands missing the two fingers lost long ago in an accident on high-tension wires. They were very much alone up there now, and their daughter, sons, other family, and friends looked on with rapt faces as they repeated the vows with the same earnestness and the same belief in the tradition they had vowed to uphold fifty years earlier. But they were not alone: All those years they had shared were grouped around them, surrounding them in much more intimate company than any crowd of well-wishers could ever have been.

I looked at them as I finished my speech, Dad spruced up with a big bow tie, my mother in a soft green dress. I would have liked to rush over and hold them to me in the all-embracing hug of a child, and pin a big medal with a long streamer of pride on them. You deserve something more. How does one encompass all those years in a few words of admiration and gratitude?

I realized our privilege in sharing the celebration with them, how rare it is becoming and rarer yet it will become. We had such fun preparing for it, enjoying the occasion to be together again, to see all the family, but it was much more. I had the distinct feeling of being a long-distance runner in a relay: We, the three married children, were now taking up the long tradition and carrying it on. I don't know if this was sentimentalism, or the feeling people naturally have at golden weddings, for this is the only one I've ever attended.

Knowing how fragile marriage is, remembering how my parents had seen us all through shaky years when one problem or another was testing our marriages, our commitment, I wondered where we would be ten, twenty, fifty years from now. But I only wondered for a moment, for there they were, a testimonial to enduring solidarity and love. I accepted being a runner, being part of the relay, feeling the kinship, the tradition.

I was aware of the differences in our marriages, of the separated time frames life had set us down in. Even with the confirmation of the longevity of marriage that their celebration gave me, on that day I still thought about the differences, how the pressures of today—to be equal, to fulfill oneself—had affected my marriage, the marriages of my friends, how we had had to withstand mobility, the media, changes everywhere. My parents had lived a life without the questions and stresses we had had to face, without the options we had. My parents had faced different problems, hadn't they?

I never wondered *why* they had endured, buttressed by convention, duty, and their religious faith. They just had. Yes, they loved one another, but weren't they also a habit with each other? I resented somehow, then, the fact that they had never had to question their marriage; that long life of routine had made them so sure of themselves, so sure that there was never any question that day would follow night. It almost seemed that we lived in two different worlds.

Four Years Later

Going back to their home this year was different, and I realized that earlier I had been so quick, so rash in my judgments, so blind in my perceptions that I had ignored the essential under my very eyes. Now, four years later, I was looking, not for the differences, but for the fundamental things we all shared, the bedrock foundations that were common to all our marriages—mine, my parents', my brothers', my friends'—no matter what the differences in our lifestyles or behavior in marriage.

This time, other things too have changed. My parents are older now, and show the fast changes that four years can bring to those over seventy. My brothers are older as well, heavier; their children, nine between them, have grown to young adulthood. We are all older now, and our concern for our parents is greater.

I notice that Mother listens to the radio and rarely turns on the television. She tells me the sight in one eye is failing and only a cornea transplant will help. She doesn't want it; she's had too many operations. I notice that Dad is doing all the work in the house, the cooking and the shopping. He takes me aside and tells me not to mention it if I find egg on a spoon. "Your mother can't see that well now." He's rearranged the house, moving their bedroom into the dining room so she won't have to climb the stairs. I look at my father and see the way he cares for her, his devotion expressed in a thousand small ways, and the household tasks now devolved upon him.

Since his retirement ten years ago, they have had a good life—secure financially; enjoying trips to visit their children and friends, winters in Florida, new friends in their senior citizens' group; keeping the house in shape, always making improvements. My husband and I had planned to invite them to come to Europe with us this year, to visit our son in Portugal and then to take them where my father has always wanted to go, to Rome. I wanted him especially to experience this, to fly in a plane across the Atlantic and see the world he has always been so curious about. After all, his time is running short. How many years will he have to see the amazing variety of life, to discover the new and the different?

Now I know that he won't go, no matter how we solve the problem of how to care for Mother. She would be welcome in either of my brothers' homes, but my father's trip to Europe and the Vatican will never materialize. But I know his steadiness, how he wants to be by her side, that this is his responsibility, and that no opportunity, no dream, could ever be stronger than the bond he has with her. How could one imagine living any part of life without the person who has been somehow part of your life for more than fifty years? He would feel uneasy, that he was being unfair. Ten to one, if he did go, he would want to return home after the first week. It saddens me that neither of them will experience it.

And Mother—looking at her I am anguished at the way her age and illness have incapacitated her, at seeing this woman whom I knew when she was so full of life and interests, snap and vigor, whose whole world of sensing is shrinking now. She would deny it; she would not even articulate her fears about her failing sight.

She says, "Oh, no, I can't go to Europe. I can't even get to church sometimes. Of course your father can go, but I don't want to leave here. I don't want to go to David in Georgia. Maybe I could stay here in Akron with Jerry and Joanne." But she says it without conviction. She doesn't have to say that she is sorry for holding him back. She expects his devotion and he gives it, not out of guilt, not out of duty, but out of love. She cared for him and devoted her life to the family through all their lean years, scrubbing and cooking and ironing in the normal way; now it is his turn to care for her. They have cared for and taken care of each other throughout their married lives, and now it is no different. That is simply what marriage is for them. The things done for one another, the love, are not accounts to be balanced daily; caring and love and obligations are evened out over the long years of a lifetime.

And so the sadness I feel may come only from my own perspective. Yes, they are dealing with the problems of aging, of caring for each other with the limitations and debilities of age. But they are still loving in the same old way, not above an occasional jab at each other for the idiosyncrasies they know so well, still making the occasional fond compliment, and being honest toward each other in a way that perhaps only those who have been together for more than fifty years can afford.

I see the touch of heroism in my father's unsung acts of love, but like many others, my father would laugh if I called him a hero. He knows only by the pat on the arm or the longer-than-usual hug I give him that I understand him, and admire him.

I feel an indignation rising against the feminist who categorically downgrades all men. As a woman I know that women have had to take domination, that we have had our futures determined without our say. I know that our marriages have been a perpetuation of submission and our opportunities limited by men in a man's world. But there are also men who live up to honorable expectations, who love in the fullest sense of the word, who give up their dreams, just as women give up dreams, in exchange for the less glamorous but enduring rewards of raising children and keeping jobs. Who hasn't given up dreams? Who ever has them all fulfilled?

I am astonished yet sustained by my mother's attitude. She tells him to go, but knows he won't. She hasn't the least shred of guilt. Why should she? The question of whether she would do the same never enters her mind. Of course she would. Even in my sadness, and in my bitterness about what life deals us, I marvel, I am uplifted, by their attachment. I think of the hippie oldster who shucks his job and family and takes off for the commune or art colony, the woman who leaves her home and children, the doctor–husband of a friend of mine who left her the day she came home after a mastectomy. I wonder if what these people find in their compelling search will ever match what I see in my parents' lives.

"Marriage," comments Malinowski, "presents one of the most difficult personal problems in human life; the most emotional as well as the most romantic of all human dreams has to be consolidated into an ordinary working relationship which, while it begins by promising a supreme happiness, demands in the end the most unselfish and sublime sacrifices from man and woman alike."

Contrasting the unswerving connection my parents have had in their lives with all the options and opportunities—and uncertainties—we have today, I can understand the discontent, the changed definition of sacrifice and duty and obligation, the impelling desire to live the varieties of life we know exist before it is too late. The individual is precious—truly irreplaceable—as an entity, and yet only equal in importance with the unities he forms with others.

We are no longer expected to sacrifice ourselves, our total beings, to marriage when it threatens our dignity as persons. No one is expected to stay in a destructive relationship—for instance, the wife battered by her husband, the husband demeaned by his wife, crushed. No one expects a wife to immolate herself on her husband's funeral pyre as was once the custom in India. These are seen as savageries today, violations of human rights. When seen in this light, the small sacrifices we make in our close and loving relationships become simple demonstrations of caring, our gifts to commitment. There are times when individual welfare becomes inseparable from the common good, both in society and in marriage.

My parents' marriage, the fifty years of their memories and ours that we celebrated, remind me that marriage and fulfillment in life do not come for free —not because of sacrifice but because of caring, not because the partners try harder and harder, but because they have love for each other. My parents give me a warm reassurance that two people can care for each other forever, that the virtues and values we have held as human ones are still alive and well, that we can go on coping somehow, helping one another, our loving and caring achieving dimensions we never thought possible.

The common good of my parents' lives *is* their individual good, for although with every choice of one thing, we give up the freedom to do another, at the same time we gain the greater freedom that our conscience and good feelings about ourselves give us. My parents reinforce the absolute knowledge that they matter to each other more than anything else in the world. Their love has survived incident after incident, compromise after compromise; it has been compounded of alternating disappointment and joy, of giving and receiving, until they are so bound together that not even death will separate them.

Such bonds, and especially such mutual dependency, are regarded negatively today; it is felt that something must be wrong with marriage if it fosters such reliance on another person. What about freedom? What about the individual? What about *me?*

I believe the answer to those questions is that although we have given up many of the traditional structures and expectations of marriage—and, after all, our marriages exist in a different context from that of my parents—we need not give up marriage itself. The concept of marriage is flexible, so that today it can stretch to accommodate the new "you" and new "me," because it is being made by, and for, the "us."

I understand now the full meaning of commitment, of the time together that marriage implies, of being the most important person to someone and having someone as your most important person, of the context of family in which it all takes place. Neither of my parents has lost individuality through their marriage, traditional though it is. If anything, it has reinforced their distinctions to me as individuals. Their attachment to family and to friends is an extension of their commitment to each other. Their problems and sadnesses are part of their happiness, neither detracting from nor amplifying it. Life doesn't deal out happiness evenly; it's not something we have as a birthright, but it is there for each of us to make a reality, translated into our own terms in life.

5

House of Marriage

I came back from my parents' house to my own home nourished, reassured, feeling the flow of my life from these roots in my past, sensing the genuine connection between my marriage and that of my parents. I knew that our lives were different, but that we were living them on common grounds.

I was glad to be home in my own order, back to the life my husband and I had made for ourselves—our apartment, the books, the frayed Mexican rugs, all the things that surround us and remind us of our life together.

Simone Weil has said that order is the primary, the essential need of the soul. Amid the disorder, the confusion, the turmoils in our present world, there are few things left that give order to our lives. Marriage, for me, is one of them. Marriage has given me a sense of order in my life, as it has in my parents' lives, and in the lives of my brothers, old friends in Akron and elsewhere, and the people I speak with every day in the course of my work.

Clearly, marriage is not the only way to order a life. I know that I could live without marriage. So could George. We each have sufficient resources so that we are not dependent on the other for identity and meaning as people. More and more people are choosing not to marry at all, or to marry much later in life. But to me, and to millions of others, marriage has provided a sense of place where we feel at home in the world.

We build that place, our House of Marriage, in any of a multitude of forms, according to our needs and desires and abilities. My parents built theirs from tradition, as if from sturdy stone and rough-hewn beams, a house of marriage almost identical with their neighbors'. Many people today still feel secure in such a house—the blueprint drawn by habit and patterns of the past, the size of the rooms prescribed, the house marked off into territories.

Others, like me, need more flexibility. We want to make some rooms larger, remove or shift walls, change the furniture around. We want to be our own architects and build our house of marriage to our own design. Some will be houses of glass, full of sunlight and airy. Others will have solid walls of concrete or brick, or gabled roofs; some will be geodesic domes, penthouses, or rustic shacks surrounded by flowers.

No matter how different your house of marriage is from mine, each one, each marriage, I believe, rests on five foundation stones. They are—

• Primariness of each partner to the other, each being the other's most important person.

- Intimacy, not only physical intimacy, but the way we open and reveal ourselves to the person we marry.
- Connections and the network of family, the ties created by a marriage to other families, past and future.
- Continuity in time—the sense of building a history together over a span of time; and the way we come in time to know one another so deeply.
- Responsibility to the commitment we make when we marry—to our partner, to ourselves, and to the family we create.

Some marriages may place more weight on one or another of these ordering principles, but unless all of them are built in, in some way, the house does not stand. Take any one of them away completely and the relationship changes from marriage to something else.

These are the bedrock fundamentals that my parents took for granted and trusted instinctively. We in the seventies might look at them again to be reminded of what remains solid after the radical social changes we have come through.

There are of course many other elements, which we use in varying proportions, in building on those foundations: love, interdependence, loyalty, mutual respect, honesty, friendship. The style in which all the elements are combined gives each marriage its own particular character, but, in my view, unless a relationship incorporates all the indispensable foundations, the basic premises of marriage, it cannot be called a marriage.

What about children? Certainly they are a substantial part of most marriages and were at one time the most important premise for marriage. Though for many couples children are not a necessary part of their lives together, where there are children, they always serve to reinforce and enlarge our commitment, and remain today, as they have always been, one of the greatest responsibilities and rewards in marriage. And yet, for the parents, unless it is lacking some of its foundations, the marriage remains after the children are gone.

Different styles and different goals in marriage do not alter the basic truths of our lives together. We need to recognize that these foundations enable us to make our marriages strong, workable, and satisfying, that they buttress our love, trust, and fulfillment. Knowing what we have at the foundation, we can repair chips and cracks, or if need be, we can understand why we must leave a house, and be able to leave it without guilt, when its foundations have crumbled beyond repair.

According to astrology, once a marriage is sealed, it is thenceforth ruled by the Seventh House, the House of Marriage. In moving into our House of Marriage we are destined to be changed, not by the heavens, but because we have chosen to share our place in the world, to join our lives in intimacy.

6

Marriage Makes a Place

"Marriage is like an island," says one couple.

Another disagrees. "No, not an island; more like a peninsula. You have this identity, but it's attached to a greater thing, to society and the community, and you're a part of it in addition to marriage."

A third says, "It's more like an apartment in a large building. There's much more interaction, but you have your own little private place to pull into."

What kind of place is marriage? Most often it is a place you know the way you know your home. It has the comfort of familiarity; it is a place where you can be yourself, where you have the ease and security and time to fulfill your needs. It is a place where the deepest intimacy is possible.

One of the greatest differences between yesterday and today, between my parents' marriage and my own, may lie in our need today for greater intimacy in our marriages. Intimacy in marriage encompasses all aspects of knowing each other, from how many lumps of sugar he likes in his coffee and how bad tempered she is in the morning to our most passionate merging in sex. But today intimacy has come to mean even more. It means the sharing of our inner souls, becoming so close, so open to each other that we experience the deepest communion and knowing of each other.

George and I talk more, live more deeply, share more aspects of our lives than I think my parents ever did. We have a greater need for sharing our inner selves with each other, and for working out, through this intimacy, the many more choices and problems we have. I see this in many marriages today. And while I know that there are people who may not desire great inner intimacy, and that good and stable marriages do exist without it, I have come to believe that this sharing of self beyond the routine of living, and beyond our sexual merging, is one of the most important components of contemporary marriage. This intimacy helps us to meet change and grow, to reorder our lives, to remain aware of how our unity transcends our individual concerns.

I lie with George out in a field in South Dakota, wrapped in a blanket, looking up at the huge arc of the night sky dotted with the lights of the universe. We hold hands, trying to comprehend the wonder of the infinite together, swinging into the contemplation of life and eternity, swinging back to our own earthbound personal intimacy. There are times when we cannot see this larger vision together. The sky is clouded or our vision is clouded, or we are caught up in the mundane laundry of our lives. This intermittent rhythm makes the flow of our marriage: together and apart, absorbed or distant, from the particular to the general, from the sky to the earth. From a contemplation of the universe and the larger scheme of things, to the security of the private and personal intimacy we share in this place we have made for ourselves.

We can look at marriage in very simple terms and talk about the way we share our daily lives. Jane knows the way John uses his fork and which sock he puts on first. He knows what time she wakes up in the morning, and how much she hates to do laundry. She knows he always leaves things until the last minute and gets angry when she cries. We know the twisted toe or the mole on the back. We come to know thousands of little things about each other in the daily round of our lives. This is the easy intimacy that has the comfort of familiarity and habit, that helps make the wheels of life go around smoothly. "I can't imagine getting up in the morning," says one young woman, "without that cup of coffee my husband brings me." A husband says, "We're both morning people, our inner clocks are the same, I guess. And perhaps that's why we get along so well together."

We come to know all sorts of things about each other, and try to adjust our lives so that all the pieces of our day-to-day existence fit together. "I'm a neat, compulsive person, and she's not, so I do the dusting and vacuuming and wash the windows because I know she hates to do it. But she does all the bills and the checkbook. I used to do it when we were first married, but it drove me crazy, so she took over."

Couples share information with each other on this level of intimacy, information that is not usually highly loaded emotionally, or threatening. They share mundane secrets about themselves: small comments on the day's events, plans, triumphs, anxieties. "Jane and I went to a movie today." "I'm really worried about Jimmy at school." "Gee, I got a real kick out of seeing Charlie today when he stopped in at the office."

Affection and love can exist at this level. They can be expressed in little ways as well as large ones. This kind of intimacy is almost an essential of marriage, and couples have always enjoyed the warm companionship that is expressed by this comfortable familiarity. You're at home, in your favorite bathrobe, there's a hole in one sock and it doesn't matter.

Many couples are satisfied with this degree of intimacy. It is not risky or threatening, and for many reasons they have made a tacit pact that this is all they are going to share with one another. Sometimes earlier, sometimes later in the relationship, they reach their maximum threshold of disclosure. For some couples, it would be like breaking the sound barrier to cross onto a new level. They may go on in this easy way for years perhaps, until they hit a snag, have a problem, or run into serious differences they can't resolve, something that requires more of them than they are accustomed to give. If familiarity is all that is left, there is no newness to share; there is, ultimately, loneliness and boredom.

If part of our place of marriage is made up of the trivia of living, another is made up of that particular intimacy that has always been associated with marriage—sex. The major intimacy in marriage was always thought of as sex, and, in general, sex was for procreation, although there have always been people for whom it meant love and pleasure. Genital sex was a functional obligation of marriage, legally and morally; children were needed as workers for economic survival, to ensure cultural stability. Even when the economic need disappeared, children were still considered the reason for sex. Sex in every society has been guarded and circumscribed in some way.

Today's sexual revolution, however, has taught us that sex is also a way to express our deepest emotional needs. With developments in contraception, and with new concepts of the roles of and relationships between men and women, sex is no longer restricted to marriage. Sex is in marriage and out of it. We are exposed to it on television, in books, in magazines, in advertisements. People have premarital sex, sex between, during, and after marriages, casual sex and serious sex. But no matter how common a currency it is, sex is still a most powerful drive, and the sexual intimacy of marriage has not diminished in importance. Sex is still central and fundamental to marriage: It is our most complete way of expressing our love, our merging of me and you into us. And in the creation of another human being, it combines the two of us forever in a genetic link.

Sex is demonstrable intimacy. We know it happened. Because it can be the very most intimate expression of our love and commitment to each other, it becomes as well our expression of loyalty and fidelity to each other—ideally, that is. In reality, sex is often the barometer of our relationship, reflecting how we feel, how things are going between us. It varies with all the nuances of our physical and emotional states. It can be used for or against, it can be constant or variable, boring or exciting, it can be mono or stereo. Because sex is so variable, the other aspects of our physical intimacy take on more importance: the tenderness and affection we express in caressing and kissing, touching and holding, walking hand in hand. Sex in contemporary marriages is not an end in itself, but part of the greater intimacy that enables us to survive and grow.

A thoughtful young couple described to me the dimensions they feel sex occupies in their marriage.

Liz: The sexual part of marriage adds something to our relationship that you don't have with others. It's a new dimension, which we don't have in friendships. Some couples do, but we don't. I think sex adds a very rich kind of dimension, and it makes you want more in return; you're giving more of yourself.

Larry: The sexual part is very important, it's basic, and you don't have that with your friends, your colleagues. Sex is the meeting point in our relationship. We work a lot more things out through sex than we realize. A lot of times we get really tense from daily tensions of living and working, and sex brings great relief. It really brings you close together, and from there you proceed to being soft and nice to each other and being able to talk. But I don't mean that sex should be an escape from problems. You shouldn't depend on it to get you back together if you've gone through a period when you've been alienated from each other. You shouldn't have to have sex to be able to talk.

Liz: I don't think sex will solve basic kinds of problems. But it doesn't always have to be serious. It can be a kind of escape, a pleasure. I'd rather have a nice evening of sex than go to a boring play or a bad movie.

The place of sex in Liz and Larry's modern marriage seems to me to represent just how our various intimate needs draw from all parts of our lives and reinforce them. Our desire to be known is one of our basic human needs. In the past, much of this need was met with a variety of relationships. In small-town American life, we had many close bonds and contacts besides our marriage that gave us back the reflections of ourselves we needed. We had family nearby; we lived in a familiar neighborhood, with shopkeepers and clubs, with clergy, with schoolteachers who may have taught our parents. A place where everyone knew everyone else throughout their lives. Even big cities had neighborhoods, many of them ethnic in origin, which reproduced small-town life in the midst of skyscrapers and department stores.

Today, all that is changing. Our lives are more fragmented, in cities and small towns alike. We may or may not know our neighbors. We know that the friend we make today may be gone tomorrow—consider how large corporations routinely shift executives and their families from one side of the country to the other after a handful of years in one spot. Remember how easily, with the promise of a new job or a different career, a household is packed up and disappears overnight. The shopkeeper's business folds. The local grocery store is replaced by a gigantic, impersonal supermarket. We move to a new community, leaving grandparents, parents, aunts and uncles on the other side of the continent. We have fewer and fewer threads of continuity in our lives, continuing contact with fewer and fewer people. Today, as never before, our marriages are assuming more responsibility for fulfilling the need to be known, for providing continuity in our lives.

We have our conversations over the dinner table, we have our expression of intimacy in sex, but in our lives today we need a deeper kind of relating in our marriage to help us function in a world of fluid social relationships. We need a place in our marriage where an emotional intimacy is possible, where we can share with each other crucial insights about ourselves and thus where we can reinforce our individuality in an impersonal world at the same time that we strengthen our unity as a couple. We can only create the climate for this intimacy and trust in each other in a place where we have the freedom to be ourselves, where we are accepted, and encouraged to grow. Marriage, with its foundations of commitment, loyalty, and responsibility, with its comfortable familiarity and physical closeness, is for most of us the place where that intimacy is possible.

In their marriage Jeannie and Ray have had more than the usual ups and downs, but it seems that the downs have been weathered just because of the special feelings of intimacy and sharing they have had from the beginning of their relationship.

"Ray and I come from families that neither of us were completely happy with," Jeannie said. "I certainly had a lot of misgivings about my own family, and I felt very not OK about myself and them. I felt they didn't want what was best for me, and I think Ray felt the same way about his family. In essence, by marrying each other, Ray and I became each other's family. He became my grandmother and my grandfather and my parents, and I became his. He gave me permission to be me. This is the most exciting part of our marriage, that we've got permission from each other to be ourselves. We know all the things we've wanted to do and be, and everything we've been, the secret things we've never dared tell anyone else. He's the only one I can tell all this to, absolutely and honestly how I feel. I felt very lonely until I met him, and when I met him, I had something that made me feel not lonely. We share so many things that I'd feel lost without him."

Intimacy is easy when we are people sharing similarities: We both like jazz and walking in the rain; we love skiing, loathe crowds, and can't bear pistachio ice cream. Sharing similarities is the solid basis in a relationship from which we go on to build new self-extensions. But it is another thing to face sharing our inevitable disagreements and differences, to be intimate in conflict and through conflict. Can we still be intimate when we clash over our differences; can we be intimate and love each other in anger, hurt, or depression? It is precisely through these crises, through the exposure and acceptance of our differences, both desirable and undesirable, that we grow and mature. In a very real sense, the intimacy we can gain through facing and resolving our conflicts makes it easier for us to dissolve our fear, our doubts, our inhibitions, our anger. And then knowing better each other's strengths and weaknesses, knowing we can grow through conflict, we can go on in greater trust to risk sharing other confidences about ourselves and our feelings.

Beyond accepting each other we have a need to learn about ourselves and our partner in ever deepening ways. I realize that it is not just the risky sharing of our inner thoughts and feelings that is important for a bond of deep intimacy, but the cherishing of that revelation, having the long-term assurance that our confidences about ourselves—those that make us so vulnerable—will be respected.

"The thing that really frightened me about marriage," one young wife told me, "was that you are really so totally vulnerable. That person could kick you in the stomach. But after a while you know that you can trust each other and can even do things that are completely crazy and he'll still love you. You also find, at least I did, that you are not so vulnerable after all."

No relationship can sustain the pressure of intense intimacy a hundred percent of the time. While I am convinced that most of us could benefit from and need this deeper intimacy, I also believe it must be balanced with our need for being apart at times, for exploring and growing in other areas, for renewing oneself and coming back to intimacy with our partners enriched and replenished.

In recent years we have been bombarded with cries for freedom, for total honesty in all our relationships, and in the process, I think, we may well have lost our awareness that some courtesy and some self-control show our concern and love as much as telling all the truth all the time.

Dr. Yael Danieli, a family therapist, analyzed it very tellingly. "We've lost an awful lot of the old traditional structures and rules on how to interact, what to say, what not to say. I think people are very frightened of the freedom we have, and feel very anarchic about it. They're saying, 'Now I can do everything, so now I can say everything,' and they do, under the guise of 'I'll be frank with you. . . .' The result is that people hurt, mercilessly, and expect the person who is hurt to take it and not respond in a hurt way. It's frankness to the point where if anybody says to me today, 'I'll be frank with you,' I say, 'Please don't. Be considerately honest.' Frankness is saying, 'You look terrible today.' Honesty is saying, 'How are you doing today? You seem troubled, you seem tired.' With frankness, you are naked of concern or consideration."

Too much honesty can take its toll on marriage, and what starts out as a mutual exploration of our inner selves can turn into, as one disillusioned divorced person expressed it, "dumping on the other, all in the name of honesty. It wasn't nice at all." We can learn how to return to a more sensitive understanding of each other in our honesty. Where else can we be as honest as in the safety of marriage, where we are known and loved? A high degree of honesty goes into good communication, mutual understanding, and trust. But there are always parts of ourselves that cannot be shared with or verbalized to another. There must always be some degree of consideration for the other.

As Tim, the Boston advertising man, puts it, "My wife and I are open with each other. We're honest with each other. But there are certain things that are better left unsaid. I mean, if I see a good-looking broad on the street, I don't go home and tell my wife about it. She knows I admire good-looking women, but I know it would hurt her if I told her things like that. There is a lot of openness in our marriage, but there's a lot of individual privacy, too. Everybody has a private side, and I think that's right. I don't expect my wife to tell me everything that went on prior to my meeting her, or every thought that ever entered her head, but if she feels like telling it to me, OK. But there's no hiding of things, either, and I don't think there's any hiding of emotion. If you're angry, you're angry."

We have a responsibility to respect the vulnerabilities of our partners and not to betray his or her trust. Laurie says of her husband, "He can tell me things that are even against my family, things that are true. My mother does eat like there's no tomorrow, and he can tell me that, and I won't be offended. But he also knows where to draw the line—not because it would be improper to say something, but because he knows there's a certain loyalty that I owe my parents, and a certain loyalty to my family that he recognizes.

"We know secrets about each other. There's nothing I can think of that if I said it to him he would reject me, but at the same time, I like knowing that I can still always hang on to me. What it boils down to, I guess, is that even though I feel that we're together and that I can count on him, we might be alone one day, even just by death, and I want both of us to know that our confidences are respected. For example, I don't want to know the special things between him and his first wife, not because I'm not curious and not because I resent them, but because that belonged to her, and now, this time belongs to me. I don't mean in a possessive sense, but it's mine and it's special. I don't want to feel hesitant about the things I confide in him, and I would never want him to, even if our marriage shouldn't work out. I wouldn't want him not to be able to enjoy another woman because he felt that I had taken his confidence and betrayed it. And if he did that to me, I know I could never trust another man the way I've trusted him."

In good marriages, we may sometimes haggle, sometimes hurt each other, but we know that in the long run, it will even out, that if our caring is constant we can meet our problems together. Intimacy in marriage enables us to meet the world, to restore ourselves, and to help each other know who we are.

Hal: I hope I give Della a sense of self. I know that she gives me that feeling of autonomy. When I feel like I'm falling apart, she's my biggest cheerleader. She'll come to my rescue, and in that way, she really gives me a reaffirmation of myself. I hardly feel I'm losing myself in marriage—only gaining. The best part of marriage is being known by someone else. I can come home and just know that she will know where I'm at, and I will be able to tell her where I'm at. We can really talk, and I can be held or I can hold her.

Della: It's the same for me. I come in from a day when everything has been rotten and miserable and my head is spinning, and I can lean on Hal. He's like a wall that can fix it all up and throw me out again, like a sounding board. It's not that he is doing it *for* me, either. He's there to help me put it all back together. He can embody my good parts and give them back to me and say, "Hey, do you know what you're doing?" And I bounce back again on my own, renewed, a little different each time.

Whether we view our marriages as islands or peninsulas or some other kind of place for sharing our lives, there is an increasing need in today's world for the confirmation of self that we search for in marriage. We can no longer take things for granted about our marriages; we need to articulate clearly how each of us feels, what he or she wants, or is trying to say. I have always felt that my marriage could not have survived without that kind of intimacy, our marriage having grown out of special circumstances and premises, and in a place quite different from that of my parents.

I was the gypsy in my family, and the outward contrast between my parents' life and my husband's and mine has always caused a lot of tribulations. I was always chided for never settling down, for reading too many books, for spending our hard-earned money on our work instead of a house, for dragging the kids around for whole summers or whole years at a time. But my husband and I never felt the need for a home anchored to one plot of ground. We lived in tents, campers, motels, in reconverted army barracks, apartments, and large houses abroad—wherever we were, with our children, was home. The focus of our life together was not to ground ourselves in one place as my parents had, but to do the things that interested us, and to work together. Not that we didn't try—our files are full of plans for unbuilt houses—but the pursuit of our interests in people, in anthropology and archaeology, and the necessity of making a living kept us too busy to build a home. An apartment in New York did just as well. Because we have traveled and lived in different countries where we were "foreigners," and because we live in a big, impersonal city, we came to expect more of each other in some ways than the more settled couples might, and in other ways, less. We didn't have to be measuring our life against an arbitrary standard. I felt no compulsion to be the proper wife; George didn't feel pressure to be the proper husband. We could be ourselves. But because of the circumstances of our life, the stresses and pressures, the options and influences so vastly different from my parents', for example, we have had to become even more intimate.

George and I come from widely different backgrounds, too, and our marriage has been filled with laughter—and tension—in the meshing of our two different points of view. At times it is a magnetic attraction; at other times, a pain in the neck. But we have been pushed into greater intimacy, it seems, by exploring the differences in our backgrounds as well as by the pursuit of our collaborative goals in life. The stresses of our existence are immediate and frequent, and we have found that talking, arguing, fighting about them, and working through to a solution, gives us the mutual support we need to meet our problems. We cannot, even now, take things for granted.

The greatest difference between marriages today and those of yesterday is, I suspect, that articulation of our feelings, that sharing of emotional intimacy. No matter how different our styles of marriage are, there are always love and conflict, frustration and elation, happiness and sadness, tragedy and joy. There are always problems to be solved. The place we create, where we live out our marriage, can change to fit the circumstances of our lives and the times we live in, but the foundations must remain the same.

7

The Most Important Person

Who comes first? Who gets the first dance, the most concern? How do we define our loyalties in marriage?

A young woman told me, "My grandmother used to say to her children, 'You're mine and I love you all, but your father comes first.' I don't think I would ever say that to my children because it can't really be good for them, it demeans them. But I think one or the other has to be first in your mind and my husband certainly is ahead in mine and I am in his."

This sense of primariness—of being each other's most important person—is a strong foundation of the House of Marriage, just as much as the physical and sexual intimacy, or the networks you tie into when

57

you marry or the history you create together. Primariness is the essence of pairing, and from it come trust and loyalty.

Being primary can be expressed in many different ways. For example, "I know that whatever comes up in our life, he would be the first one I would turn to." "If you win the Nobel Prize, who are you going to call first to tell about it?" "When it's your birthday, who do you want to hear from first?" "My wife's my biggest cheerleader, I can count on that." "I know that my husband is never going to knock me, even when I'm not around. Being primary is knowing that if someone attacks you or makes a joke at your expense, your spouse will defend you, no matter what."

Primariness does not mean that the person we marry is more important than ourselves. The consuming passion in a romance that places the loved one on a pedestal, higher than oneself, is a short-lived illusion. The longing to lose ourselves in another person has inspired poets, artists, and songwriters through the ages. "She for him had given her all on earth, and more than all in heaven." "You are to me everything." Deep down we know that we can become too attached, and this can become possessiveness. There is a world of difference between belonging and owning. However closely two people may become entwined in marriage, they always remain separate and distinct beings. By choosing one person out of all the world as the most cherished, the most important, we do not have the right to expect the impossible of him or her, or to rest the whole weight of our needs, fears, and insecurities upon that person. Sooner or later, the one who feels possessed will want to struggle free, even at the cost of losing love and breaking out of the marriage. "What I really dislike in marriage is possessiveness," a divorced man told me. "I think this is an evil that will rise up and destroy the relationship. It did my own marriage. We all feel possessive at times, but it can get to be abject and undignified.

I don't want the feeling of being owned or possessed. I want the feeling of being desired for me, being desired wholly and completely by one person, but not being possessed to the point that it will restrict me in terms of giving back to that person."

Because marriage does join our paths together and form us into a unit with certain kinds of exclusivities, choosing the person we marry implies that for the time being there is no other person who means as much, with whom we would rather live. Though there are other reasons for marrying—mere convenience, social or parental pressure, because our friends are doing it—more and more people today are consciously choosing marriage even though there are a large number of other possible life-styles. The feeling of being primary in importance to the person we do marry has to be behind that choice if the marriage is to become the sustaining base of our life.

For many of us, the primary relationship with our partner in marriage provides us with the security we need in order to interact confidently and successfully with the outside world. "A good marriage gives each one an anchor," says one woman who juggles motherhood, marriage, and career. "It provides a kind of stability, emotional security that allows the other one to soar. Maybe the best way to describe how I feel is by its opposite. I have the feeling that sometimes when that security is denied, people suddenly find they aren't performing so well on the outside, in their jobs, in their social relationships, in their feelings inside themselves about what they can do."

Knowing that you are primary and that only one other person is and can be primary to you is also a means of recognizing your freedom. You know who's on first, you have ordered your priorities in the scheme of things. A young woman lawyer has found that after she got married, "I never thought again of whether I was going to have sex with other people. And before I got married, even when I knew I was getting married, I was conducting affairs with several people at different times. Now I've been married two years, I go on business trips with men in my capacity as attorney, and I have no interest at all in other men as sex objects or in a possible affair. In fact, it's nothing but a headache and it interferes with our lawyer–client relationship when he tries to make a pass at me.

"A lot of men who are now my friends are ones I had affairs with. Now they're strictly friends, and that's the way I want it. I realize now that even before with sex, I didn't want to be that close to them. Well, I don't have to be, and I'm not. My husband gives me that closeness I want. I keep my distance from a lot of people, and I'm much happier. Marriage gives freedom to me in terms of my relationships with other people—there's a lot more ease and comfort this way."

Sometimes primariness is seen in a gift, a decision, a willingness to do something you don't want to do because it is important to the person who has your greatest loyalty. Both partners of a young couple I met in Canada have demanding jobs and a variety of separate interests, so they have learned to make concessions when it comes to deciding how to spend their free time. "If something is important enough to you," the wife feels, "then your spouse should follow through and be there. It happens in my marriage. For example, we belong to two boating associations and they have annual dinners two weeks apart. They're deadly affairs as far as I'm concerned, especially when you get these avid iceboat racers talking about the Frostbite Series and let's get a Ladies' Series going this year. But I go to the dinners, and I listen, and I make my little input, because it's important to my husband.

"But sometimes when your ideas and his are different about what's important you have to sit down and work things out. My husband's idea of a supreme holiday is to go to the Caribbean and sail for two weeks on a forty-foot boat. I think that would be poison, worse than going to a couple of boring dinners. So last year when he wanted to go, I said, 'Fine, get some other people together who want to go, and I'll make a reservation for myself at a resort. That way I can be in the sunshine and not have to sleep on the boat, which you know I don't like.' We left together and came back together and we were both happy.

"On the other hand, if somebody offered me a great job in New York that would be thirty hours a week and paid $65,000 a year and I had to sign a contract right now, I couldn't do it, much as I might love to. My husband is established in Canada, and I owe it to him to discuss it and to see what the potential would be for him if we did make such a move. And I would expect the same from him."

The decisions that many dual-career couples have to make today often test the primariness of each partner to the other. Sometimes they work it out by taking turns in choosing priorities, even moving their home in accordance with one partner's job demands and then with the other's, if that is necessary. Some have found new solutions, such as long-distance or part-time marriages. It may be harder, but it is certainly not impossible to remain married and primary to each other even when living together only intermittently. Military service and other jobs that involve long separations may not allow what we consider the optimum in married life, but they have been managed by many couples, couples who are willing to make the compromises because they are the most important people to each other, together or apart.

The primary feeling we have for the person in whom we have the greatest trust, with whom we share the deepest intimacy, is in a different category from the devotion and even passion that we give to achievement in a profession, in the creative or performing arts, or an absorbing career of any kind. One kind of importance often complements the other; without either we would be lacking an essential part of our lives. A painter I know put it this way: "My art is important to me, but without my husband I'd be obsessed with loneliness and nothing could fill that void. Art would not be enough for me. If you're a person who doesn't feel that the world is confused and scary when you don't have some one person who is first, that's OK, but it's not me."

Newlyweds are visibly of such primary importance to one another that it sets them apart in their own exclusive world. There is an early need to protect the relationship while the couple are getting to know each other and developing patterns of intimacy and inter- action, and while they are melding histories and de- ciding where life is going to take them, there is always, and necessarily, an element of exclusivity in singling out one person for the most attention, the most care and concern. We *have* married one person; we *have* declared with this act our mutual destiny and our interdependence. Of course, after the early stages, marriages also can grow into too much exclu- sivity, too much togetherness, cutting off the friend- ships and many activities and contacts we need to live fully as individuals. No one person, not even the most important one in the world, can fulfill all our needs.

"I'm sometimes confused about Don and the chil- dren," a young mother confesses. "Who comes first? I'm more torn about it than he is. I'd say definitely that he loves me more than he loves them, but I can't say that for myself. I love the children, not equally, in a way, but I just can't say that he's always first. Don feels jealous of the kids some of the time; in a sense he's a rival with them. But in the end I'm looking forward to living with Don without the chil- dren, and I know deep down that I'd drop everything and crawl to Alaska to be near him if that's what I had to do."

However adoring and adored, compassionate and important to each other you and your partner are, a child is a part of yourself and also primary in your life. Each is equally important, each in a different category. Children need not displace the primary relationship between husband and wife.

Parents have a different kind of primary relationship with their children, and there are times when the children have to come first. Each child deserves to be cherished and respected as the important and special person he is. Parents nourish the child's sense of self-esteem and self-worth, just as married partners reinforce those things for each other. At times children require more of our attention and support. As one young mother remarked, "Unfortunately my husband can't be first with me in terms of time right now, because the children are little and they demand a lot of my time and attention. But you never lose sight of the fact that children come and children go, and your spouse is there forever—or you hope he will be. I think good marriages are like that.

"Of course, you have lots of periods when you're having children when things go to hell, like your relationship with your spouse. It's really hard to include your husband in the early mothering. For example, when I started nursing my first daughter, I had a kind of funny feeling—I didn't know if I was my mother nursing me, or my daughter nursing her daughter, but I knew that I was one in a very long line of mother to daughter, and obviously, it was hard to include my husband in that. But the point is, at a certain time, you put that baby in another room, and go and spend that time with your husband, and it will be all right."

Primariness in marriage can be demonstrated by little actions—a look, a gesture, an indefinable glow in a smile—as well as by great sacrifices. It is as abstract as loyalty, or as time. Knowing that we are the most important person to the one we love is a continuing current in our lives together. Like the flow of electric current, it is there even when the lights are off. We don't have to spend twenty-four hours a day with our partner to show that he or she is first in importance, anymore than we spend twenty-four hours in bed to show that we are intimate, or twenty-four hours worrying about our responsibilities. And of the time we spend together in marriage, the quality is more important than the quantity.

The quantity and quality of time vary from couple to couple. For most of us, primariness does not mean spending all our free time together; that would be too much togetherness. Some couples do spend most of this free time together, but much of it may be spent in boredom, bickering, not communicating, not sharing, not feeling the current flow even when silent, reading, or watching TV. Others spend a great deal of time apart and still maintain a vital marriage, because the time they do spend together is of the highest quality, when they share with each other intimacy and closeness and activities they care about.

When a supposedly secondary relationship—a parent, friend, or even work—becomes more important and takes away too much time, energy, or affection, primariness between husband and wife is seriously threatened, and the hurts and recriminations start to pile up.

Jane is twenty-nine and has one small child. Her husband is a restaurant manager, who spends most of his time away from home, at his job, socializing with his men friends and even guests, and, Jane discovered, conducting an affair with a co-worker. Jane is miserable, almost to the point of breaking up her marriage. "I'm secondary in every respect," she says. "I'm secondary to his friends, to his work, I'm secondary to him even in respect to my son. He kisses my son first when he comes in the door, not me. And now I'm secondary in bed, since he's had this affair. I'm secondary to everything. Like I said, I feel like a piece of furniture. I wouldn't have to be first with him all the time, just once in a while. Even the counselor told me, 'Your marriage is dead. You're standing at a graveside, so walk away. What do people do when they go to a grave? They grieve for a while, and then they walk away. You don't stand at the graveside and cry and weep forever.' He says, 'Your marriage is dead,' and yet on all sides everyone is saying, 'Isn't there something you can do?' I can't resurrect something from a grave. What do they expect me to be, Houdini?"

Primariness cannot be defined in negatives, by listing the things that detract from this quality in a relationship. It is a positive feeling from the heart that is confirmed in a thousand small ways, or perhaps only in a few important ones. If it is there, you know it, however it is expressed. Primariness is not a cut-and-dried allocation of time. It is a devotion, a cherishing, and a genuine caring for the other person that no hours on the clock can measure and no amount of rules or specifications can codify. It is hard to keep a marriage alive without it, but with it, we are enriched, secure; we have a real awareness that we are not alone.

8

Connections and Kinship

I remember how, as a very young girl, I used to sneak into the darkened parlor of my grandmother's home on a hot summer's afternoon. Grandmother would be baking and bustling over the big wood stove in the old Pennsylvania farm kitchen. I would pull aside the velvet curtains and draw up the dark green shades. Then out would come the old albums of photographs and the boxes of tintypes. I spent hours with them, enchanted by the strangers looking out at me, immersed in the mysterious history of my family, surrounded by the musty smell of the seldom-used parlor.

No one answered my questions about these oddly

dressed, stiffly posed men and women. Reticence was a virtue in those days. Never tell the scandals, only the good things, what you don't know won't hurt you. But I knew even then by the sparkle in this one's eye, the coquettish turn of that one's high-buttoned shoe, by the surly look on a mustachioed face and the grimness of clenched hands, by all the details that photographs reveal, that life wasn't as simple or as virtuous as my family would have me believe.

Now I am here again, forty years later, sitting on the floor, literally surrounded by my network of family. My brothers are here, aunts, uncles, parents, cousins, in-laws, all sitting among the suitcases of old photographs sprawling open. Albums, tintypes, long rectangular frames of family reunions cover the tables and floor. We are all together; the twentieth century mingles with the parade of venerable ancestors in their Hatfield hats, jumpers and flouncy skirts, watch-fobs, handlebar mustaches, long beards, and high-necked dresses, marching across the wide pyramid photographs of four hundred people joined together in blood and marriage, animosity and love, grief and joy.

We look at log cabins, horse and buggies, big farm-houses half-buried in drifts of snow, summer picnics and hayrides, and Model T's. The family joins in, laughing and remembering, spilling glasses of beer and passing the crackers and cheese. Then, sober and quiet for a moment, we recount the deeds and quali-ties of one or another, this aunt who was a saint, that cousin who was a scoundrel. My uncle jumps up to pound away at the piano as he did when I was a youngster in smocked dresses and leggings. We all sing along, and I am carried back to my childhood.

Now that my connections are welded together by time, now that I have a long history of my own be-hind me, I've found out all about those old photo-graphs. I know of secrets and sadnesses, hilarity and outrage, cowardice and constancy. These people were real. They were devoted, tender, callous, flighty, stubborn, independent, sturdy peasant folk who had their share of both rapscallions and heroes. They were the people I came from, sensible, serious-minded Midwesterners for the most part, my heritage. I feel nourished and comforted; I feel the meaning of the word *kinship*.

I had the same feeling of connections when George and I listened to his parents' stories of their youth, looking at their old photographs. I can hear his mother laugh now as she explained each picture—in Guatemala, in old New York, herself while a young bilingual secretary, eating lunch in the park with a parasol and a floppy Victorian hat. Here is her young and poetic caller in a stiff collar, George's father. Here are long rows of relatives in Spain, Puerto Rico, New Jersey, and Peru. Here is George in his long christening dress, or scowling in knickers and Buster Brown haircut, and the two of us at our wedding, the merging of two totally different backgrounds, George with his Latin expansiveness, emotional and volatile, and his Irish charm, and me with my Middle Western practicality and warmth and our shared belief that nothing was too hard to accomplish if you set your mind to it.

I feel closer to the present we share because of this filling in of the past, enfolded in the gentle and spread-out network of our families. But warmed and reassured as I am by the experience, it makes me more aware than ever of how alone couples can be today in marriage. Many of us no longer live anywhere near our families and see them only once in a while. Reaffirmation of our connections from time to time like this is a refreshing drink from a wellspring. Ultimately each of us has to create and live out an individual history. I live a long way from those farms in Pennsylvania, a long way from my childhood in

Akron. We are a long way from Spain and Peru. And yet I wonder if the rows I hoe in the big city where I live are all that different from those on the farm. Is the way we solve our problems really different? Aren't our emotions and feelings the same?

In marrying, we pick up our destinies in a large album of kinship and family. It is this sense of jumping into a time frame of place and connections that distinguishes marriage from other forms of living arrangements.

"I think one of the reasons I married my husband," says Martha, who has been married a couple of years, "was that he could stand my family. I have to spend a lot of time with them, and my husband is an angel about it. When you're just living together, you often avoid even meeting his family, never mind getting close to them.

"I think you can judge someone by the way he treats his family and your family," she goes on to say. "I look for goodness in a mate, just a basic biblical kind of goodness. I judged my husband that way. His parents are people of very modest means, and he's always helped them."

"I married my wife, I didn't marry her parents," the young husband says. But in a sense, he has. Someone once said that there are six people in a marriage: the spouses and two sets of parents. In-laws, of course, can quickly become out-laws, but they are a fact of married life, whether you embrace them, ignore them, love them, or hate them. At its best, family expands our capacity for love and responsibility. We admire and respect our spouse's parents for themselves or because they are a part of his or her life, a link in the chain of personal and family history we join when we marry.

"My mother-in-law when I met her was just a sickly little old lady," Hilary told me a year after she was married. "But I was looking through her album of pictures of Len, and there was her own picture as a ballerina thirty or forty years ago. She'd been a professional dancer, and she'd never mentioned it. Ever since then we've talked about her experiences, her past, and now it's something special we have between us. I know we don't have her for very long, her health is failing, and I feel that this is something Len and I will have later. Our children will have that sense of history, of roots and origin, and they'll know where their father came from. That's why I like marriage. There's a history, a lineage, there's something more than just today. I'm not talking about living in the past, but it's something that makes sense out of where I am today, and why I'm doing what I'm doing."

Parents can reject a daughter's choice, a son may disappoint and alienate his family by picking someone they consider unsuitable. We all know stories of couples who have married in the face of strong family opposition, who were "disowned." Yet there are easily as many, or indeed more, marriages that succeed despite vastly different family backgrounds. Despite the differences, the couple ties in to the networks.

"I'm in a strange situation," Judy said to me. "I'm the only Jewish person in the middle of a bunch of Irish Catholics. I'm not like Dennis's family at all. And I know from what his mother has said indirectly that she sort of resents the fact that I'm Jewish. Maybe she's afraid I'll influence her grandchildren against her, which is nonsense. But at the same time, when you're married, no matter what kind of crazy different backgrounds you come from, you're really a part of his family. I love to hear everybody telling stories about Dennis when he was little. It makes me feel that I'm really sharing his life."

These young women, who are only at the beginning of their marriages, already sense the importance of their connections with family, of their roots, and of the networks they have joined. I think that part of the reason their very new relationships seem so solid is that they have begun building their history and their House of Marriage from that foundation.

And there can even be unexpected benefits, as Judy found:

"My father couldn't get used to the idea at first that his baby was getting married. Even though they knew Dennis already and liked him very much, my father was very quiet for about two months after we announced our engagement. I have one brother, and he and my father don't communicate well. Once my father got used to the idea of Dennis and me getting married, he suddenly had someone to replace the son he could never communicate with. He and Dennis like to do a lot of the same things, and now they're always off doing some project together."

For Hilary too, something extra was added to her relationship with her own family by her marriage:

"Since I was eighteen, I've not been very close to my sister, and now that's changed. She adores my husband, but I had never cared for hers. Now I see her husband in a different light because he and Len get along so well, and I see my sister in a different light. Len has brought me closer to my family in that respect.

"When I go to visit his parents' house, I see the tree he climbed when he was a little boy, things like that. It gives me a sense of his history. His parents are his history, and his family albums, and the crazy aunts. What I love is that he's a product of everything they did to him. If they hadn't been the way they were, he wouldn't be the way he is. He wouldn't exist, in a sense."

But what of the couples we all know who reject their families, who cut off their parents and connections completely? Does that mean those couples have eliminated the foundation of family and kinship from their marriage, and thus do not have a marriage at all in the sense that I've been talking about? We know that is not the case. In many such marriages both partners are successful and happy. Their families are still with them, however, if only as models of what they do not want to repeat in their own marriages.

Connections also move forward, as Ray feels with his strong sense of history in the making:

"When Jeannie and I got married, I said, 'My family begins now, and everything in the past is nothing,' because that's the way I feel about my relatives. My grandfather on my father's side was a rat, and he still is. My father's an alcoholic, and each of them in turn treated his son in such a way that he grew up to hate and fear his father, ending with me. I feel that I broke this pattern. I have a good relationship with my son, and that's important to me. I've read that these things are inevitable and the pattern can't be broken, but I've proved that it can. I changed the script I inherited, and it was a lousy script to read.

"I do have a terrible temper, and I yell, but my father yelled louder and he hit. He demanded a kind of martinet response from me and his other children that I don't demand from my children. I can see that my son wants to be with me. I couldn't get away from my father often enough."

Then, conscious of what the lack of connection with family has meant to him, he adds, "I have several friends who would come to my help a lot faster than anyone in my family, but I'm not happy about that. I don't want that to be my children's fate. I want them to have that connection with their family that I never had."

Another young woman, who has what she calls a domineering mother, comments: "I remember my husband wanted to apply to the University of Maryland graduate school, and I said, 'No way. It's too close to Virginia. We're not going to get that close to my family.' I need my own freedom from them and to maintain my own identity away from them, from my mother."

Her husband, however, says, "When we got married, I did think in terms of family; I think that was a factor in our relationship, that perhaps sometime in the future or maybe even at the moment, we both might feel the need for getting more into roots."

Donna and Jim have been at loggerheads for years over relatives. He revels in his family get-togethers. She hates them, both the get-togethers and the relatives. He would like her to enjoy the parties as much as he goes, but since she can't, they've made a pact—he goes, and she doesn't. "It's her loss," he says, shrugging his shoulders, and it may be. He, incidentally, has willingly taken on his wife's widowed mother as a joint responsibility.

We make our adjustments as they are needed, realizing that no matter how attenuated our connections with family are, they are still a legal fact and a strong influence in our married life. As Margaret Mead has written:

"Every marriage re-enacts in a thousand ways the early-childhood scene, especially the division of sex roles between mother and father. Whether these parental roles are imitated or flouted, they are always a factor in marriage. Everything the two partners ever felt through their long and happy, or unhappy, childhood is there to be reviewed and re-enacted. . . ."

Our parents' heritage, then—their past—is also a part of our present, in many of our attitudes, habits, likes, and fears. What is more, whether we choose—and it is our choice—to turn the family links to good use as support networks (if not in the sense of financial or physical support, then at least in the sense of attachment to the past), or whether we reject them outright, for good reasons or bad—whatever the choice or necessity, every couple in marriage is by definition beginning a new history, building it out of the days and years together, out of shared experiences.

We begin piling up our own pictures of our time together. We can add them to the albums of the two families stretching behind us, or they can serve to record the connection that begins, as it did with Ray, right here, and which will develop into the sense of continuity that underpins a marriage and projects it into the future.

9

Time of Our Lives

Marriage is a commitment to time together, all kinds of time. When we marry, we do so with the words "till death do us part"—an assumption of forever. There is a sense of a future, the continuity of hours and days to be spent together. The value and quality of the time we spend together in marriage supports the relationship. It can enhance our understanding of each other and ourselves. Marriage is time that can last to the golden wedding, a lifetime. It can be, and often is, the short or long span between the ceremony and divorce. Among the foundations of our House of Marriage, it is the one we take most for granted.

What happens to time in marriage is a matter of

circumstances and how we play out our lives. Time can be ignored, overrated, undervalued, forgotten, or treasured. Some of us are paupers in present time; we exist only in the future. Others try to hoard time, afraid to spend it, while still others hang on to the past, and lose the moment today that will shape the future.

Each of us in a marriage plays games with time, yet it is the one commodity we both have an equal share of. Time in marriage means not only hours and days and years; it means all the loving times, the moments of gloom or of utter peace, the angry scenes, the same old jokes. It means the time to slough off habits, or get over hurts, or cultivate the slow-growing plant that is trust.

Because we have spent so much time together, my husband and I share a range of emotions and experiences neither of us shares with anyone else. Even though I would like to wish away some of the bad times, I know that they had value in teaching me that I could survive them and grow through them. The passage of time is the only way we can find out what we really have in a marriage, and the only way we can learn about one another more deeply. Time allows me to see more clearly where I am because I know where I've been.

My parents married forever, no question about it. Even with today's increasing divorce rate, *forever* is a word one hears constantly from young people just starting married life as well as those who have been married long enough to know that marriage has its seasons and cycles.

Margaret is an artist who for nearly forty years has combined her work with her marriage to a prominent public official. "I certainly expected to be married for good," she says. "When I was young, people got married forever, or why did you get married? I had the feeling of getting married forever very strongly. I had divorced parents, which hadn't worked out very pleasantly for them or me. And I've had a very happy marriage. Of course, I liked the idea of being married in the first place. I wanted to be placed, attached to someone. I don't mean 'a place,' but I wanted to have a connection with someone who belonged to me, and I've been lucky in that respect. I think you have to count a little on luck in marriage.

"Looking back at myself and looking at young people today, I think all young couples must worry. It's all so new. You're more self-conscious. Are we doing all right? Is this how it should be? And who's to tell you? Your parents had different lives, your contemporaries have different lives, and you only see the surface. What goes on in your house is different from what people see. But if you've lived together a long time, the way my husband and I have, then you know you're getting along, you're doing things right. When you get to be my age, you're a little more peaceful about things. You can say to yourself, about a boring party, for instance, that this evening, too, will end, just like other bad parties. And the same is true of rather more serious things that happen. I think the fact that you've survived a lot of things together makes you appreciate that you have somebody around that you like."

Besides her work, Margaret's life has included motherhood, grandmotherhood now, and many social obligations resulting from her husband's career. "As you grow older in a marriage," she says, "you do different things, and you change gradually; your responsibilities change, and the way you use your time. You're freer in a way. You have the same ties to your children, but they're gone, and you don't have to be there for them every minute. We've always liked spending our free time together. My husband has always wanted us to have evenings to ourselves, to have a chance to talk to each other. We've had more opportunities to do that in the past few years, even though we're both busy with our work. Of course, there are other moments when you separate and do things by yourself, see friends he doesn't particularly want to see. But there are still all those other times when you're going to be together as a couple. I guess that's really what forever means, knowing you're going to be together."

Not everyone is so lucky. Time does not heal all things. The seams do crack in many long-term marriages, and "forever" gets to be more of. a burden every day.

Some old friends of the family come over to visit from time to time. When they do, the kitchen table becomes an arena of strife and anguish. After forty-five years of marriage, Dan and Edie are facing the proverbial empty nest. His retirement hasn't settled well with him. It has left him high and dry. He is one of those who spent his life, invested his whole identity, in a corporation job, and now is unable to enjoy his leisure or to get himself started in something else. He wants to repair TVs, or sell real estate, or, well, he just doesn't know. Edie had a series of operations which kept her tied down, but now she can race around energetically again, the way she used to. She wants to move to Florida, he doesn't. For years, their children's problems kept them involved and demanded all their energies. Now that the kids are managing on their own, now that the job is gone, now that the house is empty, without all the old necessities clamoring at them, they have to face what they have left, themselves.

Neither Dan nor Edie ever learned to understand the other through the language of intimacy, except for conflict. But they hold all the weapons long familiarity has given them, and so they fight, raw emotions and anger and misunderstandings spilling out all over the table. After all these years of pulling together, they are now pulling apart. Now, when they have the time to enjoy what they have earned, their dissatisfactions and yearnings and built-up angers are coming out, in such ways as drinking too much, or having tragic brawls.

They seem destined to pass the last years of their particular forever without peace, without ever knowing each other except in hostility and despair. Because they have been together so long, they are likely to be even more miserable apart—separated or divorced—than they are now. Time, like other elements in marriage, has its perils, when the only intimacy left is that of old enemies.

Of course we know it does happen that a relationship runs its course, and either ends or becomes destructive. We know it can happen at any time—after a year, after five years, or even after nearly half a century. Still we marry with the hope that we are going to make it. "Forever" remains our symbolic commitment to time in marriage, even when we hesitate to admit it. "I did not marry forever," says one recently married young woman. "I married thinking, well, if it works out, it will be great. But it may not work out. Now, after a year and a half, I think it will be forever, but I didn't go into marriage even daring to tell myself that it could be."

"I married forever and a little longer," says another young wife. "I think relationships last if people are honest with themselves. I was a little threatened at first by the idea of forever, I admit. I thought I was going to have to cram it all into one day. I look at it differently now after being married a couple of years. I know I'm going to be rocking with my husband fifty years from now, so I'm going to live today the way I want to live today. I can wait for my fiftieth anniversary because I have a lot of things to do before then. On the other hand, it's easy to say I want to be happily married for fifty years, which is what all of us say, and it's another thing to say that I know it absolutely. I *don't* know it in that sense, but I feel it inside."

Marriage is not like an intermittent affair or a one-night stand. With its commitment to the space and continuity of years in which to grow and develop our rapport and ourselves, marriage is quite different from the emotional intensity we may find in a short relationship.

And for all the excitement and richness of a brief encounter, it is still only one point on our time continuum, a bright bead that hangs apart from the others on the chain from past to future. It's true that we *can* love someone instantly. Some people do fall in love at first sight by some internal magnetism as yet unexplained by chemistry, magic, or computer technology. But whether the relationship continues will depend not so much on the intensity of the first attraction as on the time and continuity the couple will share. Only time together tells us if we can stand the inevitable disillusionments and go on holding on to each other in times of indecision, anxiety, frivolity, sorrow; whether or not we can stand aside while one or the other fights his or her own battles. The continuity of marriage gives us time to develop a mature love that does not fluctuate with changing circumstances, or the seasons, or the latest whim or fancy. Only through time can we know our limits, and our constancy.

We learn to use the time we have in our marriage to grow in our emotions and understanding. Elaine, a very contemporary young wife, finds that "sex flows more out of circumstance, more out of the situation, when you're married. Sex when I was dating came more out of the lack of time—you didn't feel that you had that time, it was a rush. In marriage there are no limits. Whatever happens, happens, whenever. It also means that you don't always have to play a whole tennis game: You can just serve sometimes if you want to. There's a lot less pressure."

We need time to explore the depths and heights of our feelings for each other. "I find much more intensity in our relationship as the years go by," another married woman says. "Naturally you don't feel passion every day, and it's not a constant plateau of feeling, but it's something that grows over the years you're together. It's the ability to express your deepest feelings, and it has to do with a lot of emotional states, not just sex. I'm glad we've had the time to let that happen."

In the course of time, we see each other transformed by the experiences of living. As Dr. Lewis Wolberg, a psychoanalyst, observes, "You relate to your mate in various ways, on multiple levels. You relate as a sexual partner, as a peer, as an authority figure, as a symbol of a parent, as a child where you become the authority, as a projection of yourself and your idealized self-image. You have to work out these idealizations and unrealistic expectations. Just in the course of living together and in working through whatever these blocks in your maturation may be, in order to get along better with your mate, you find it involves growth within yourself—a genuine growth experience that gives you ultimately a realistic picture of yourself." It is this opportunity for growth and maturation that time in a marriage gives us. As we share time with each other, we become something different, and yet we remain the same. Like our physical bodies, where every cell is replaced every seven years while our general form remains much the same, marriage offers us both constancy and change.

We are influenced as much by societal changes as we are by our personal growth cycles. I don't know that anyone has an easy answer for how to mesh our individual passages through growth with our growth as a couple. There are snags all along the way. Not the least of these is our expectation that our relationship will always be happy, smooth-running, without hitches. But there are hitches. If we recognized that these cycles and phases are not easy, but can be exciting and rewarding, we might not be too hasty to dump relationships when our rates of growth are different.

Change—isn't that the key word of our time? There are changes all around us, technological, scientific, societal. Changes in the relationship between men and women, in attitudes, in the differences between our lives and our children's. Even my parents have changed through the years, mellowing, accepting attitudes and things they never could have imagined or tolerated when younger. It is a measure of the strength of their marriage that they are still changing and growing.

Terry is a typical modern woman in her schooling, marriage, and family, in her having undertaken some serious activity outside her marriage—namely, free-lance writing. She has thought about what she wants and sees her goals change as the expectations of women in our society have risen.

"At one time when I was in graduate school, I expected someday to be a French professor," Terry told me. "I had one grueling year of it and I was miserable. I finally got the gumption to decide that this wasn't what I wanted to do. It was my first failure, and half my identity went out the window. Then I realized that I was a different person from the person who had entered graduate school."

Terry had already been married a couple of years by the time she stopped her graduate work, and she had recently had a baby. "At first, I had been positive that I was going to have a career while I raised my family, but I found I no longer wanted that. I wanted to be very free-form, to fit in my career with every stage of my life. As my children got older, I would have more time and would therefore work harder and more seriously. I still feel very much in the process of finding and discovering. The children are only two and six, and I don't know where I will end up in ten years, but I'm convinced that I'll do something. The point is, I feel very strongly that there is as much space as I want within this marriage for me to do whatever I want. If I wanted to go out tomorrow and go to medical school or law school, I could find a way. It wouldn't be easy, but I could do it, and Gregory would accept it if that's what I wanted. He might have qualms, but he would find a way of making it work. We're agreeable and accepting of the changes we want to make. We've come to the point where we've realized that we are going to have to fulfill ourselves, come hell or high water, and we'd better find a way of making marriage viable with all that that entails. I think a lot of men and women our age feel that way."

Gregory feels that "the basic responsibility in marriage is the notion of continuity. Otherwise, what is the meaning of marriage? Why do you need a contract for something that won't exist tomorrow? You're committing yourself, not to something that is in a recognizable form now and will be the same next week. You can't make a commitment not to change, to remain static. People aren't going to be the same in twenty years, but there is the idea that the two of you will grow—not together, which is meaningless —but we will grow and we will live together, and we will do this thing called life together."

How much time do you and your partner spend together in your marriage? The average American spends more of his or her life with one spouse than with any other human being. But what is the quality of that time together? It is claimed that the average couple, for all their time together, spends little more than twenty-seven minutes in the span of a week talking to each other about themselves, or about more than the simplest exchanges over necessities. How much time you have together may have very little to do with the essential quality of that time, or with the continuity of the marriage. Must it be on an everyday basis? Some couples do spend every waking and sleeping hour together, living huge quantities of their lives in each other's physical presence, yet the quality of the time spent together is very low; their being together doesn't mean anything at all, really—there's another warm body over there in the chair, and it might be any warm body. Other couples can spend very few hours together and be completely happy, each sufficient unto the other.

George and I, over the years, have spent a considerable amount of time together in the pursuit of our work. It has been a good and productive use of our professional time, and it has contributed to the strength of our marriage. And yet I wonder if it hasn't been too much time together. As close as he and I are, I find that I still need time to myself, as most of us do, for pursuing interests of my own that mean little to George—seeing my own friends, for example, or having solitude in which to work alone. We all have periods when we don't want to spend our time in the usual way or when we need to be alone.

There's time left over, though, after you've taken care of the fundamentals of existence, jobs, the housework, attending to the needs of children. That time left over is discretionary time, which you can use however you want to. That is when the quality of the time is more important than the amount.

Lynn and her doctor husband, Doug, don't see much of each other. In addition to his daytime duties at a large metropolitan hospital, he's often on duty at night in the hospital's emergency room. "If he ever left me," Lynn said, "it would probably take me a week to figure out what had happened—hmm, it's Thursday, and I thought he was coming home by Monday."

Although they don't have long periods of time together, Lynn and Doug make sure that the time they do have is high-quality time, a time when they share intimacy and closeness.

"He comes and goes, but I know he'll come home sometime. And he will be coming home to me, so I'd better make it count. I bring the world outside the operating room to him. We really don't have that much awake time together. I suppose if we have ten hours a week, that's a lot. There's nobody I'd rather see than my husband, and given a choice, we'd really rather spend our evenings with each other than with anybody else. But it's also agreed that I'm entitled, whatever that means, to time to myself, away from the children. That means baby-sitting, and that means he pays for it. I think a lot of husbands err in not spending ten or twenty bucks a week in baby-sitting time to give their wives freedom to do whatever they want. It's such cheap money—twenty bucks compared to half an hour with an analyst. And it makes all the difference in the world how two people feel together. The other use of baby-sitting money is to buy us time alone together, out to dinner or maybe just for a walk."

Some people share some high-quality time with a confidante, or a friend, or a lover, and a lot of low-quality time with their partners. Those people have neither a marriage to the friend, because it lacks the other elements of a marital relationship, nor a full marriage with their spouse. Certainly, we need some of that high-quality discretionary time with friends as we do for ourselves alone, but the marriage is weakened if time with others becomes more important. The best thing, of course, is when the two people in the marriage genuinely enjoy their time together.

We share time in marriage, different kinds of time —hours spent over the breakfast table, special times we spend alone together, times of deep spiritual and physical intimacy. We share in the history of our families and the history we begin creating for ourselves when we marry. My marriage, like my parents', has been the slow accrual of one event after the other, each one colored by the others. We can't rush it; we can't build the House of Marriage all of a piece. The only thing we have for sure is the present moment

and our past. We all have a span of time unrolling
before us on which to write the history of our relationship. If we do not value time in marriage, we are
the losers. Time and place together give us the space,
and the untouched strip of film on which we alone
etch the development of our relationship.

10

Responsibility

People who can satisfy their needs without intimate primary relationships have no need for marriage. They have no need to share in the mainstream of a continuing relationship, where mutuality and inter-dependence define the structure. If you are not going to be interdependent, why marry?

Time was when interdependence was mainly eco-nomic. The husband went out to work while the wife kept the house and minded the children. He supplied the income, she supplied the support system. His-torically and anthropologically, marriage was an in-stitution for cementing the ties and reciprocities between families and societies. It ensured the protection of the child, regularized sex drives, and provided for inheritance and economic survival. Everyone worked together; the family was the basic productive unit. The woman was dependent on the man for economic reasons, the man was dependent on the woman to run the home and care for their children, additional hands for work. With the development of industry, production moved out of the home and marriage began to change. Women started to move into the labor market and economic survival diminished as a coercive force in marriage. Economic pressure on and within the marriage altered over time, and the balance of our interdependencies was tipped toward satisfying the expressive needs of two people in marriage. Personal growth and the intrinsic value of human relationships began to be predominant in marriage. One of the clearest demonstrations of the flaws in a purely economic approach to marriage, reaffirming the importance of its expressive aspects, is the fact that even though women can and do become economically independent, they still marry. And they marry for the reasons we will always marry, to fulfill our very basic emotional needs. It was Engels who first said that when women became self-supporting, the only reason for marriage would be love.

Nowadays, we are interdependent in ways other than strictly economic ones—in terms of our roles, our emotions, our tasks, in socialization, in child rearing. A woman who has a successful career is not economically dependent on her husband, nor is he on her, but they still are interdependent emotionally and socially. There is a flow and exchange in interdependence that takes into consideration each one's needs.

The kind of interdependence we have in marriage today rests on the foundation of responsibility and commitment. Marriages are no longer held together solely by external coercion; they are held together more by their own internal cohesion—by love, by being primary to one another, by intimacy and companionship, by the time we have shared and expect to share, and by our sense of responsibility to each other and our children.

Responsibility runs like a common thread through all the good marriages I see. In my parents' marriage, certainly, it was demonstrated in evident care and caring for each other—as I have seen it in many other marriages, in young marrieds, in more contemporary and open marriages. Caring for each other, balancing each other's times of trouble with pleasure, caring for each other's welfare and the children, being genuinely supportive. As my friend Paula Gould said, "Marriage gives you a special intuition—when you walk in the door and get together at the end of the day, there's almost an instantaneous decision as to who has the prior need tonight; you know whose problems or needs are more important, there is an instant knowing that tonight you or I will shelve our own problems for the moment and help the other. It is this putting aside of self at times that is the essence of caring and devotion in marriage."

We establish our commitment through defining and choosing our responsibilities, through defining the particular conditions of our own marriage. Commitment can be demonstrated by duty to externals, to what others expect of us, to a house, social standing, children. But today commitment in marriage is focusing more on the internals, our needs for personal growth and caring, for determining our joint goals and common purpose, sharing our interests and our inner selves. The commitment to stay together and work out all these needs through the inevitable difficulties depends on many things—one of them is having the time to build a way of living together, and to know each other through many different experiences.

When you get married, you do give up something— your fantasies of those infinite possibilities that gradually change as you make certain decisions about your lives together. Both George and I felt it was in exchange for the purpose we shared, a dream we had in common, a life of sharing our personal growth and responsibilities. The big question, of course, is how much do you have to give up? Where does responsibility to self become less important than to the other, and the marriage? Is it a delicate balance that needs constant adjusting, or do they overlap?

Carole, who is a markedly independent person, expressed some of the ambivalence a lot of today's young married people feel. "My responsibility to my marriage is just to be the best person I can. *Free* is a word I like to use, just to be a free kind of person. I don't like any kind of roles or role expectations, and I've never been very good at accepting them. It's important to me to think I have the freedom to do anything I want to. I have to be me. But I would turn it around from there. My responsibility to my husband is to give him the freedom to be a person, too, to let him be himself."

There are some things, however, that we should not assume as a responsibility in marriage, and one is to believe that we are totally responsible for making our partner happy. We are responsible for our own happiness, for our own feelings and emotions, for our actions and our responses to life that sometimes slump, sometimes rise to peak experiences—but we cannot ask our partner to accept the responsibility for making it happen.

Happiness is not a gift we can present at will to our spouse. We cannot think and feel for another person; we have no control over the inner life of our partner. Of course, we can and do contribute to each other's happiness; we can make the contribution of our own happiness to the general fund. We can create an atmosphere of trust and cherishing which is conducive to happiness, but if we think that we alone are responsible for making our partner happy, we deprive the other of his or her identity. What is more, if we make our partner responsible for our happiness, we are giving him or her the power to control us. We are negating our responsibility to ourselves as human beings. Certainly, we do things in marriage that can make our partner unhappy, sometimes carelessly, and sometimes by intent. We can also accommodate too much and become a slave to the other's wishes, and still not succeed in making our partner happy, until we come to the sudden realization that the source of the other's unhappiness is not, after all, in us, but in him or her.

A successful California executive made this absolutely clear in speaking to me of his two marriages. His first marriage had seen him through part of college and graduate school. Everyone thought that his wife, a loving, tender woman who idolized him, was ideal. She did everything any woman could possibly have done to make him happy. She had supported him through the rough years by working. She had had three children. She was a marvelous cook. But she simply had not made him happy. Her emotional dependency cloyed on him, he told me, and later, in a high-paced executive job, he found a woman colleague who took a stand for herself, who gave him, he said, something to bounce off of. She was loving, but she was tough, too, not always anxious to make concessions to him. She became his second wife.

With his second marriage, his new wife stopped working when they had a child. As their marriage slipped into a more traditional format, he found that he was now striving, as his former wife had for him, to "make his wife happy." It didn't work this time either. Even in sex, which he considered his special forte, their marriage was a shambles. He had always prided himself on his sexual prowess, his ability to love a woman, to bring her to orgasm, to give her the ultimate in a sexual and affectionate experience. But his wife resisted him, retreated, failed to respond. Then, one day, the revelation hit him:

"The day I realized that I was not responsible for my wife's happiness was the day our marriage began to get better. I had been a failure with my first wife and messed up her life. I was trying to make my second wife happy, but only on my terms. My climbing the executive ladder, managing a whole division of my company, giving her servants, cars, vacations abroad, standing on my head in bed—none of that helped. She was unhappy and I was unhappy. Finally I pulled her over one day and said, 'Look, we're both trying too hard. All the things you do for me and I do for you are never going to be enough. From now on I'm going to quit holding you responsible for making me feel good about myself.'

"Well, that was enough of a jolt for both of us to start things changing. She took a look at herself, decided to go back to work and pursue some of her own interests, and things are a lot easier between us now. Not good, not great, but getting there, and we find it easier to love and understand each other now."

If we are not and cannot be absolutely responsible for our partner's happiness, what *are* the responsibilities we take on when we marry?

Most people think first of economic responsibility, providing the income to live and providing the support systems of a home. "My responsibilities, on a practical level," says one husband, "are providing money to keep the circus going—I call it a circus because that implies fun, it's enjoyable—and satisfying my own needs and theirs, taking care of them." "And I'm taking care of my husband and children," his wife adds. "Even if I'm a lousy housekeeper, I'm there when they really need me. That's my responsibility."

Sexual fidelity, too, is repeatedly mentioned as a condition of marriage. Today, because opportunities for extramarital sex have increased, and effective contraception is widespread, sexual fidelity, once assumed on the one hand as a given of marriage and on the other as a commitment often betrayed, has now become a vital issue in many marriages. Most people want it and expect it, but they can no longer take it for granted. It is an issue that many married couples will have to face and decide on for themselves, if only to reaffirm that yes, this is their agreement, yes, they will have sexual fidelity.

The fact that men and women can and do have sex in many other contexts besides marriage affects the way we view and carry out our commitment to sexual fidelity. I have found, however, that as we grow accustomed to the new freedoms and opportunities and how to deal with them, as we become more open in our attitudes toward sex, more couples are reaffirming their need for sexual exclusivity.

"I didn't think fidelity was important," Connie says, "or that both of us would put it way, way up on our list. When we first got married, I know Paul thought it was important, but I always thought that the double standard was sort of acceptable. I really believed that if Paul was seeing some nurse at the hospital, it really wouldn't bother me. Well, now when I think about it, I know that it would drive me crazy. It would mean that Paul wasn't Paul, among other things, and I like Paul. As I know him now, he isn't capable of that, and if he did it, too many things would be different."

For some people, the responsibility of sexual fidelity in marriage is a choice they are not going to want to make. Barry, a young unmarried sales executive, says, "I enjoy being single. I don't say it's the only alternative, but in marriage, I'd be giving up personal space, my desire to do things just the way I want them. I would be giving up a kind of frivolousness that I enjoy as a single person, to kid, grab ass, be flirtatious and playful with the opposite sex. It gives me a lot of satisfaction, but only on that level. I don't confuse that with any in-depth kind of relationship I've had. I suppose I could be sexually faithful, but it would be a problem to do it. There comes a time, at least for me, when you lose interest. As far as sex goes, I seem to need the variety and stimulation of having a change in partners. So I can't imagine how marriage would work for me."

The commitment of sexual fidelity in marriage is not only a question for men like Barry, but also a question for women, like Tina, who is as yet unmarried: "I'm not sure I could ever restrict myself completely to fidelity as far as intercourse goes. I think that it will be a trend in my life, but I am not willing to say, definitely, that from this moment on, there will never be an exception. I think that to have the idea of fidelity is good, because it gives you a real basis for your marriage. You choose a partner and have plans for the future. You really anticipate staying together, and I think this gives you a positive attitude toward the marriage. You know that you would do anything to stay together, as long as it doesn't start degrading you somehow as a person or taking away other things that are important to you as well. But on the other hand, at least for me, it would really be hard, if not impossible, to build walls about myself and say there will never be an exception as far as sex goes—but I would hope that such an exception would not be really damaging in a fundamental way to whatever I tried to build up with my mate."

The concrete expression of primariness as represented by sexual exclusivity is more of a responsibility than people such as Barry and Tina want to take on. Barry also added, "I would be giving up in a marriage a kind of freedom from responsibility, I would be giving up the idea of acting spontaneously for myself."

Sexual fidelity, however, is only one aspect of the broader responsibilities people today feel they have to each other as persons.

In his marriage, Tim assumes sexual fidelity, but it is the responsibility for mutual support that he views as most important. He says, "My real responsibility in marriage has been to give my wife security, and not in terms of dollars and cents, either. Mary knows she has me, for whatever purposes, for whatever might come up. She has me to encourage her, she has me to lean on, for whatever she might need me for. She has me for a friend, someone who understands her. I don't understand everything, but I try to understand her. As for her, she feels responsible for taking care of me, and she does a good job of that, but it's more. She feels that anything I want to do, I can do. I toyed with the idea of going to graduate school, and that would mean we'd have to change our whole life-style for two years or more. And she said, right away on her own, 'Hey, that's a good idea if you think you'd be happy doing it.'

"At the same time, she can do anything she wants. Not that I don't care what she does; I do. But she's an individual, too, and I'm not about to stifle her ambition. If she wants to do something, she's going to do it, and it's my responsibility to support her and encourage her, the way she does me."

One of my childhood friends, a woman who's been married nearly thirty years, said, "There's a kind of inherent responsibility to be supportive of each other no matter what. A year ago, I had surgery on top of surgery, and it made me feel as though I had lost every ounce of femininity. My husband was responsible for making me feel very feminine, very desirable, and I think that was the reason I recovered as rapidly as I did. I was allowed three hours of self-pity one afternoon—and that was it. He realized that I had to have that time for the 'why me?' bit. He knows me better than anyone else on this earth, and he knew I needed some of it, but then that was enough."

In many ways our responsibilities in marriage in recent years have increased rather than decreased, despite the changes which might have led us to think we had shucked a lot of the old ones. A new condition of many marriages is to be equal, to have an equality of opportunity for each to grow and to expand roles, an equality of consideration for each one's needs, an equality in decision making. One university student in a class on marriage and the family told me, "I think the basic responsibility in marriage would be a combination of respect, love, and probably communication, and that encompasses a lot of things. As far as our marriage is concerned, it's nobody's *duty* to do such and such. We don't come in and say, 'You do this all the time.' Most everything that has to be done is shared—cooking, dishes, cleaning, everything. I think your responsibility as a marriage partner is to set things straight between the two of you, so that life is compatible between the two of you."

This setting things straight between the two partners is one of the new responsibilities. In the old days we were told what our responsibilities were because they were defined by tradition: The wife did this, the husband did that, and sexual fidelity was taken for granted. Today we must set things straight, define anew our contributions, how we are going to live and relate together, how we are going to change the ground rules of our marriage when we are confronted by the necessity for change.

With the changing times, we also have to juggle more responsibilities outside our marriage. There are additional responsibilities created by second marriages, children of other marriages, relationships with former husbands and wives. We are also coping, though not always successfully, with the problems of our aging parents. At one time they were generally cared for in a stable family structure, in the homes of their children. Today, with smaller living spaces making such arrangements impractical, and when both husband and wife may be working and raising children and there is no one who stays at home, couples often have to deal with the difficult and heart-rending questions of what to do with parents as they grow older and need care. And all this at a stage when there may already be a huge financial strain on the family for their children's education.

No doubt such increased responsibilities in today's marriages put greater demands on the relationship and perhaps cause more breakups, but there are couples who do manage to cope with these problems. No matter how our roles and our definitions of responsibility change, we develop and create our love for one another through the conditions and responsibilities of our marriage. Martin Buber, the philosopher, wrote, "Love is the responsibility of an *I* for a *thou*." He does not mean that we take on that responsibility as a burden, or diminish our own responsibility for self. It is our caring and concern for another that he talks about when he says, "Through the *thou*, a man becomes an *I*."

Love is giving the other the space to be his own person, his own "I." In marriage it is a responsibility for and commitment to sharing some of our personal space together, to contributing to each other's identity, to reflecting each other in honesty and faith. Marriage is a place where we can be ourselves, but it is also a place where we grow and change in personal ways through the stability of our commitment to each other. Choosing and accepting the responsibility to cherish and respect each other's beings through hardships, tensions, and joys, through personal and couple growth, through time together, enables mature love to grow between two people.

"My wife is my best friend," a young man told me, "which means that there's somebody there to encourage you in the things you want to do, somebody you can discuss things with. And love is important, corny as that sounds, the fact that somebody loves you. And you're able to love somebody back. I love my wife, and I know she loves me. It makes everything else we do possible."

What is the reality of the complex relationship that

marriage is? What is marriage really like? "If I were to tell someone what marriage is like, do you know what I would say?" The speaker is a prominent lawyer from the Midwest, who has been married for more than thirty years. "I would tell them that marriage is like nothing that you have ever entered into, that it's a different kind of thing. Unless you have a real commitment to this other person, I sure as hell wouldn't get involved with marriage, because living together with someone on a daily basis is altogether different from any kind of experience you've ever had.

"If I were to describe what marriage is like, I would talk about specific instances, and say that it's not all fun and games. But if you could look back upon the marriage you are about to enter into from the perspective of years, and relive and recapture all the glorious moments, the highlights of a married life, like the birth of a first child, and then if you could carry it on through the tragedies that befall one naturally in the course of time by being alive and living in the state of marriage, and still say, 'Yes, I accept all of that,' then marry.

"I'd cap it off by telling about the good years and the really rewarding part of marriage, when the children are grown and raised. That's the real test as to whether the marriage is built upon sand or has a bedrock of granite. When you are left alone in those later years, just husband and wife, you know whether you really do have anything in common, and whether you have put together some kind of viable life-style that truly meets both your needs. And then I would go on to describe the joys of that kind of intimate, personal experience, how rewarding it is to hear your kids' voices on the phone on Sunday, how rewarding to come home after work and share an evening together over a candlelight dinner, and talk about the things you've done today and the plans you have together for the weekend. And that's the joy and the reward of living together through the hard times, the good times.

"But if you think marriage is something you get into and out of, then you might as well make up your mind just to live with somebody or prepare yourself for a succession of bed partners, or better still, stay single, and date somebody different every night.

"When you get married, you've made a legal commitment as well as a moral one to the other person. You are taking upon yourself a legal responsibility that is distinguished from a now-and-then kind of responsibility, subject to one or the other partner's option at any time. In marriage, you're saying, 'I'm willing to accept that, I'm willing to take that responsibility.' And responsibility is the key word in all marriages—responsibility comes first, and loyalty second."

We can build our House of Marriage on strong foundations that have not altered: intimacy, being primary to each other, time, connection and kinship, and the responsibility and particular conditions we have in our individual marriages. Though some of the functions of marriage have changed, our basic human needs have not. We still need affection, love, response, recognition, respect, sex, support, sharing, companionship. Our patterns of living together in marriage may change, but the sense of order, of place, that marriage gives us stays firm and consistent. At a time when most relationships are discontinuous or short-term, marriage offers us continuity. However valuable a friendship may be, it does not have the breadth and depth possible within a marriage, nor does it encompass such a broad spectrum of shared experiences. I have friendships of longer duration than my marriage, but they are interrupted by long separations, by changes in our lives. None has had the continuity and depth my marriage has had.

If we drift into marriage without quite knowing why or what marriage means, without being sure what the bases are, we are likely to feel trapped, our illusions may become disillusionments. Without some agreement on the fundamentals, and our joint purpose and goals, the synergy of a relationship— that growth which increases geometrically by what we put into it—does not exist. Within this house we can have space and freedom for growth together, just as we do outside our own homes, from which we bring back our discoveries and growth to share. Some of the changes in our lives may mean altering slightly the structure we have built, realizing it may be lopsided once in a while until we get it balanced again, realizing there are limits to anyone's freedom, in or out of marriage.

When both partners agree that they stand on the same foundations and accept the commitment they have made, they can build a House of Marriage that is their own, secure enough to withstand the pressure of change and give them the greatest possible room to grow.

11

On the Road

We were sitting in the middle of the desert with our kids playing nearby under a mesquite tree. It was twenty years ago. We were hot, discouraged, and at a decisive moment in our lives—a turning point on our trip together to a specific destination, a critical moment in our journey together in marriage.

We had agreed when we married that our life together was to be an adventurous journey. A romantic ideal for sure. But those dreams, like all our ideals in marriage, are tested in living out the realities of life.

We were broke and the dream we had had was evaporating in the dry desert air. It had started out as our Project Flee New York. We were fed up with life in the city and with being unable to do the field work we wanted. George was frustrated with a job that alienated him, with traveling on the crowded subways, and with being a part-time father. His doctoral thesis was in limbo. Teaching was not yet a possibility, hadn't even occurred to him. There was no more money from grants for archaeology, which we both loved, or money to study until he finished his thesis. I was tired of the routine and discouraged with trying to raise two children in the city.

We decided to leave New York, take a year off for an adventure with our children while they were still young, and then settle in a better, cleaner place. We had managed to save some money. Besides, I had just written a book that was all but accepted by a publisher. There would be money coming in from that and there were articles we planned to write, maybe even another book on retiring with your children when you could best enjoy them. So we gave up our apartment, sold the furniture, stored our books, and burned our bridges behind us.

We were heading for Mexico, where we could live cheaply, explore, and do the archaeology we wanted to do. George convinced me to go via California to get a taste of it, since we had thought of settling there after our year's experiment in Mexico. Across the country we drove, visiting friends along the way, stopping in San Francisco and camping along the coast, our money running out as fast as the miles piled up. We kept buying necessities, we thought, for our year in Mexico. Then, as we left Los Angeles to head south toward the border, I received a letter. My book had not been accepted after all, and that potential income had stopped before it had begun. My agent would keep trying, was certain that it would sell eventually. But eventually was not now, when we needed it.

So the turning point was both geographical and

psychological. Either we turned off here for Mexico, or we didn't. Either we gave up or we didn't. We had two children who had to be provided for. We had our dreams and ambitions. We had no place to live, and practically no money. Even if we had wanted to borrow, we didn't know anyone who could lend us money. It was not just the present we were looking at, the dusty road to Mexico, but our whole life.

While the kids explored the desert, our arguments and recriminations shot back and forth at each other. Why hadn't George listened to me? Why hadn't we gone to Mexico first? George was the spendthrift, I was the ogre of the exchequer. Why hadn't I been more careful? What had happened to my part of the deal? We had just enough money to get somewhere, but not enough to stay there when we got there. Sure, we could get to Mexico but neither of us would be allowed to work. If we and our kids were going to starve, I'd sooner do it here than in a foreign country.

Well, there was California. Did we want to go back there? California was nice, but our fantasies of what it was like had been tempered by reality. It was expensive. Our friends lived in tract houses so close together you could hear the neighbors' toilets flushing. Our friends drove more than a hundred miles each day just to get to the supermarket and work. They had to take on odd jobs, probably to pay for all the gas. They had ulcers. Was *that* the better living we had dreamed of? Did we want to go back to New York? Did we want to go back to the frustrations and dulling routine? We couldn't return to what we had agonized over for the last five years.

What do you do in the middle of an empty, unfriendly desert, when your balloon has just burst? The dream that had kept us going through dirty slush and snow and crowded subways had turned out to be just that, a dream. George's fantasy that our money would stretch to include all we wanted, my dream that someone would publish my book and pay for it, our common dream of future experiences with our children—all of them were a bust.

Brian came over at that moment and put his sweaty head in my lap and said, "I'm hungry." Michael ran over with a beetle he'd found, and said, "Look how it shines," and opened Brian's hand so the beetle could make a trail over his dusty palm.

George and I looked at each other. We had our children, we had each other, and never mind the busted dreams and the busted finances. We began talking and forgot the recriminations, our precipitousness, our poor planning. If we could get ourselves into this crazy situation, we could be just as inventive in getting ourselves out.

What did we want to do? Where did we want to go? Somewhere different from New York and the strains it had caused for us all. Someplace away from the humdrum, where we could do our work in archaeology and anthropology and still earn a living. Maybe we should go back to New York after all. Maybe we should try California. Maybe, maybe. We were getting nowhere out there in the blistering sun, but we were working together again, as a unit, to solve our problem.

Then George remembered an article he had read in an architectural magazine some months back about large hotel corporations building new hotels abroad. He had training and experience as an engineer. "If I worked for one of those corporations," he said, "we could live in South America or wherever they're building hotels and do our anthropology on the side, part time."

And I could try again with another book—maybe about our experiences. Terrific. We'd try it. Our children wouldn't starve after all. We threw our lunch, our kids, and ourselves into the car and headed back east. George eventually got a job that took us to Trinidad for the construction of a spectacular hotel on a hillside in Port-of-Spain. We were able to work in anthropology, too, and archaeology, in an exotic, tropical country. It was great and exciting fun and hard work, and when it ended, we had to find another life-style and discuss again what our life meant and what our goals were.

That was a decision point for George and me, among many others that we have made, as we can see now from the perspective of two decades. Because our goals and jobs and directions changed so often and did not always conform to the current notions of society, we had to sit down at each turn in the road and talk about what was important to us— not what others thought it ought to be, but what had meaning for us as two individuals, apart from and in addition to making a living, having a family, being husband and wife. Because we both had more skills and resources, and thus more mobility and choices than our parents, we had to discuss more often where those choices would lead us, what the implications would be, how we felt about them and about each other. But we were better able to ride with the ups and downs because we had learned about each other, because we held each other in our disappointments, because we supported each other and solved our problems together.

We weren't exceptional or noble, maybe just a bit ahead of our time. When we married we had agreed that it would be a journey of adventure. We would be equal partners in our relationship. Neither of us would make a decision alone that affected both. We would bring up our children as people, full and equal parts of our lives. These were our premises.

My marriage and life have been different in almost every outward respect from my parents'. Their life had a fixed pattern. George and I had to work out our life in a series of changing designs. My parents had little formal education, and they had always had the same jobs. Our roles were frequently reversed, or shifted, always having to be flexible. I supported the family when George was between jobs or careers and while he was working toward his Ph.D. He has been civil and architectural engineer, researcher, space designer, anthropologist, professor, writer. I have been secretary, statistical typist, artist, community worker, anthropological researcher, writer. Each set of parents had had the same homogeneous home-front friends and family around them from the beginning. We have friends from all classes and nationalities. We started out at a time when masculine and feminine roles were still pretty well fixed, and we have come through a time when these roles and marriage and almost everything else seem to have changed.

When we sat forlornly in the desert many years ago and worked out our decision on what to do next, we were only just beginning part of a long journey into knowing each other. Though we didn't consciously realize it then, we were relying very much on the foundations of our marriage that we had already built to make the decision of that moment: our intimacy, our being primary to one another, the years we would share together, the family we had created, and our responsibilities to it and to each other. Because of our life-style, it wasn't important who was playing what role. At one time he would give up part of his dreams, part of his freedom; at other times I would give up mine. But we had to pitch in and understand, really understand, one another and what our marriage meant. We did it together, often stumbling, sometimes racing along, and frequently backtracking only to discover a new and uncharted direction we might take.

I have often thought of all the decision points in our lives and in my parents' lives. Their dependability had grown out of doing the customary, the expected thing. Their decision making had limited range, however important those decisions. Their crises left few visible changes in their lives compared with the radical alterations in the life that George and I chose. But decision making is a steady necessity in any marriage, especially in a world where definitions are changing—decisions about where we will live and how we will live, about our public lives and our private intimacies, about our roles in providing, homemaking, and parenting. Our physical beings, too, make steady demands on us as we work out how to be whole people and still be husband or wife, mother or father.

But we must remember that we are willing to undertake those decisions because we are human beings who need each other; that is why we are together. Learning about those needs, well, that's another story. We are afraid to admit them, afraid to admit that we are imperfect human beings, vulnerable, needful. It is only now, after many years of marriage, that I can see clearly that we spent the first years of our life together behind the mask of our ideal images of each other, hiding our doubts and insecurities under a kind of bravado that said, "Come on, you know we can do anything together. I'll rise to your expectations, you rise to mine, and we'll conquer the world."

We did accomplish a lot, but it would have been more honest, easier in the long run, and just as much fun if we had admitted our needs from the beginning. It is difficult enough to admit our needs and dependencies to ourselves, let alone expose them to another person. It is not easy to say, "I need you," because we are afraid the next step can so easily lead to reliance and too much dependence on the one who satisfies those needs.

I don't want to be clung to, and I don't want to cling when it is really important for one or the other of us to be free of our interdependence for a while. But I am an imperfect human being who *is* needful. I need him when I am low, when I recognize that I am bringing past hurts into my life and I need him to put that past into a different perspective for me, when I am afraid to dip my foot into the cold ocean of something new, a speech to make, a project I want to do. I need his shoulder to cry on once in a while. And most of all, I need to feel that I respond to his needs.

If I don't express my needs to my husband, he won't know about them. He has no crystal ball that tells him how I feel, no matter how many clues to my interior life thirty years together have given him, no matter how attuned we are by habit to each other's nuances of mood.

Fulfilling someone's needs, of course, doesn't mean doing the other person's work for him or her. When I started back to school at forty-odd and had to take a course in statistics, I expected George to be around to help me through the intricacies of the subject. I needed him. But he said no. He said he didn't know enough about statistics, and he had his own research to do that summer. So I felt he had let me down. But I know now that he did me a service. I had to face the fear of failure, and what I did, I did on my own. When I first stopped typing his manuscripts and reports, he said that I had let him down when he needed me, that I wasn't aware of his frustrations, I wasn't considerate of his state of mind. But I had done him a service too. He learned that he could very well deal with his own frustrations and do his own routine mechanical chores. What is more, he gained a greater respect for my determination to do my own work.

Some of his needs I can fulfill, others I can't, nor should I be expected to. Nor can he be expected to fulfill all of mine. And some needs cannot be fulfilled by anyone outside ourselves. For some needs and problems, there is no other resource. But all of us need some mothering and fathering once in a while, the solace, comfort, and reassurance that strengthen us and help us feel less alone.

What we need from our partners varies from couple to couple, and over time, every partner's needs will change. Often we need just simple appreciation, emotional closeness, and the empathy that conveys, "I understand, I'll try to be there for you." The longer we work toward our mutual goals, fulfill our responsibilities, and know each other in our trials and failures and successes, the stronger our love grows. Our bonds of caring grow stronger with each failure accepted, each triumph achieved, each small contentment shared. The sooner we admit our needs, the sooner we can find ways of fulfilling them, either by ourselves or with the help of another. The more we allow our imperfections to be, to come out in the open, the more space we can make to overcome them. The more I can accept George for what he is and myself for what I am, the more space we will create for each other to grow, to leave behind unwanted habits, to dissolve our barriers.

Some of those realizations came to me through hard experience, some through the insights of psychology and the studies of emotional needs. The movements toward greater equality and more self-knowledge and self-development have made us aware of new dimensions in life, and they have also made us question many of our basic assumptions about relationships. For most women, as for myself, new insights were gained through the women's movement. To many of us, being forced to reassess what had happened to ourselves as women in our marriages brought disillusionment, to many others new revelations of our own real worth.

I listened to the cataloguing of women's inequities, to the diatribes against the drudgery of household work. No one needed to tell me about that. Hadn't I heard my mother say over and over, "A woman's work is never done"? Yet, I just couldn't see it as *that* much drudgery. After all, as often as my mother voiced the aphorism, she always said it cheerfully and briskly, whisking the dust cloth over the furniture and sighing with satisfaction as she sat beaming at us all down the dinner table. Housework was just a fact of life. You got it done as efficiently as you could so you could go on to other things. Besides, I also saw a lot of drudgery in going to work, in getting up and stoking the coal stove before plodding out each day to an office or factory. I'd done both before my marriage.

I had always felt it unfair when I had seen marriages where the husband never lifted a finger to do any housework. And of course, I had with too little questioning accepted the household tasks as mine, no matter how much George helped. Since we lived under canvas a lot, camping out, we also thought of marriage as camping *in*—we shared the dishes, the fire making, the tent detail. On the other hand, I couldn't see it as completely unfair for me to do the housework when we lived in the city and he went out to work every day and I stayed home. I realized, though, that it wasn't just the housework, but what being allotted those tasks signified. The women's movement alerted me to those insights we all recognize now: the lower career aspirations for women, the academic and political downgrading of women, the submissive position they had been pushed into, their second-class identity in society, the exploitation they endured. I read all the books, went to meetings, and had my consciousness raised.

Most of all, I recognized the gross inequities in the marriage laws, and how society's attitude toward women affected almost every aspect of our laws and systems. Except for a wife's claim to support and some protection for the children, the law consistently accorded men more rights and privileges in marriage than women. Then I tried to see what all that had to

do with my marriage to a husband as fair as George.
A good marriage, with no obvious oppressions.

I discovered that it did have to do with me, with
all of us, with marriage, with everything. I thought of
the jobs that I had held where men were pushed up
faster and paid more than I for the same tasks and
responsibilities. I remembered that because I was a
woman and a wife and a mother, I had had to fold
up some of my own career dreams and store them
away. I hadn't thought that so unusual at the time,
but now the women's movement made me realize
that I had not been as reconciled to putting them
away as I thought. I now felt regret for those earlier
ambitions I had not yet realized. To be sure, I had
not had all the advantages and chances men have
had, but who was to blame? Men in general? Society?
Certainly not my husband, who had always encouraged me and supported me in whatever I had tried
to do. If it wasn't *my* marriage, was it marriage in
general? What I began to see more clearly was the
way our system of cultural beliefs and attitudes had
conditioned us to inequitable roles and codified behavior that locked us into typical marital roles. It
wasn't so much marriage per se but the prevailing
kind of marriage we had that said men had certain
rights and women didn't. It needed a strong head and
a balanced perspective, for me and other women too,
to assess what the conditions had really been before,
and why, rather than what they ought to have been
in the devastating hindsight of the feminists.

I looked at my life, at my husband, at my children,
and at my marriage. For a while, I had mixed feelings
about all those years of dishes and housework and the
opportunities I may have missed, but I knew that
what I had, had been good and satisfying. Sure, I had
accepted many of the traditional precepts of marriage, but not all of them, by any means. I kept remembering our own basic premises about our marriage, and I had to acknowledge that I, my wishes,

my desires, had always been prime factors in decisions about where we went and what we did. Our children hadn't kept us back, either; they had come along too. And we had shared truly and equally in our intellectual life, and in our interest in anthropology and people.

With all those considerations, I just couldn't feel oppressed either by my marriage or by motherhood. It had been too good, too exciting, too loving, too interesting, too rewarding a life for me to feel like a victim of either marriage or George.

We made the choice to have our children early, and having made that choice, and the social system being what it was at the time, we had to work things out within it the best we could. We took on a responsibility to each other in marriage, but we were adults, we could fend for ourselves if we had to. Having children puts a responsibility of an entirely different kind on a marriage. Your partner can survive without your care; you are not responsible for his life, growth, and well-being in the same way you are for your children's. Parents can cease to be partners, but our children are part of us for life.

Since I had had my children early, I wasn't faced with the conflict of children and career that so many women have today. But many women now do face a serious conflict over career and/or motherhood. To both be married and establish a career in a highly competitive world, women must often delay having children until later—and later for women has a definite biological time limit. Which do they do first, how do they do both? Some women do manage to juggle work and children, and some do it well. It can certainly be done more easily than at the time when I had young children. Still, there must be enough money and help from husband or others for child care. It is not an easy or a fair choice, even the way society is set up today. It takes a determined and innovative couple to make it work, when both work at a full-time career and have a family.

I believe that once we bring children into the world, they must take priority over almost everything else. Not to the exclusion of everything else—of fun, the pursuit of our goals and fulfillment, the primary personal relationship between husband and wife—but a priority that is a significant factor in our life decisions. If we have chosen to have children, and it *is* a choice today, then they are our prime responsibility. They are here by our grace, waiting to be molded by loving and caring. And they are with us so short a time.

If I had known during those early years how swiftly time passes, how little time children remain in any one stage—in our arms, sitting on our lap, launching out, running around—I would have treasured each moment more for what it was. For I would have been aware that it would pass, that they would move on to another stage so quickly. Once gone, those moments can never be duplicated. With the lengthening span of a lifetime, raising children is occupying a smaller and smaller portion of it.

I have gone on to do many of the things I dreamed of earlier in my life, in different ways, enriched by these experiences with my children. Where else except in the feat of bringing up children can we experience such wonderment and insights, such feelings of awe, joy, humbleness, inadequacy, guilt, and glory—the grubby hand tucked confidently into mine, some small treasure like a colored leaf proffered as a present, the three-year-old's words of wisdom, the questions we try so hard to answer, like why the moon is orange? My children have allowed me to see something old as fresh and new, as if for the first time again, because I have seen it through their eyes. We realize in no other way as we do with a child how unique each individual is and the paths each of us

follow. I have found resources in myself that I never
thought possible in meeting the challenge of my children's growth, in experiencing the delight of watching
a flight of imagination within them for a suspended
moment.

These experiences in parenthood and all the emotional and practical challenges George and I have
met as husband and wife have helped us to grow
both as individuals and as a couple.

Along with living out my life, I have been the ob-
server of all kinds of marriages and I have talked to
all kinds of people about their feelings and experiences in marriage, their struggle to understand their
own needs, the ideas that influenced them, and what
is happening to those ideas now. I have seen the
battles taking place on the home front, changes in
jobs and careers, in the marriage bed, and in all areas
of life where men and women are trying to make
adjustments to new ideals of equality.

Out of those experiences came the belief that openness in marriage, allowing both partners to find
themselves as individuals and grow from personal
strength to strength as a couple, provides the most
resilient, enduring way for men and women to build
their lives together. In *Open Marriage,* we suggested
ways for couples to achieve the equality they were
seeking through openness and intimacy and a greater
understanding of each other's need to grow.

To us the primary meaning of *open* in marriage was
and remains the partners' opening up to each other
within the marriage. The deeper intimacy, mutual
concern, and trust that can develop when two people
open their inner selves to one another enable them
to withstand inevitable stresses within and outside
their marriage. How else can we understand each
other's needs if we cannot tell each other honestly
how we feel in the caring and secure atmosphere that
marriage provides?

Another of the meanings was to be open to change.

But even when people want to change, it is difficult to break old habits and to have the courage of our new convictions, difficult to put into action those new concepts we have of ourselves, the new insights we have about relating to each other. Many people do not feel the need for any greater intimacy and openness. They are comfortable with what they have, secure in tradition and familiarity. But the changes that are happening all around are bound to affect all of us sooner or later. I believe that it is with the self-knowledge and mutual confidence that grow best through openness, that we can achieve the flexibility we need to cope with all the new circumstances and influences in marriage today.

But we must remember that, however open a marriage becomes, it must remain a strong emotional bond, a relationship of commitment. The designs of our House of Marriage may vary infinitely, incorporating new elements in with the old, or replacing the old elements with the new, but if the house is to stand for long, it must rest upon the foundations that have always upheld the union of a man and a woman.

12

Men and Women

Into the House of Marriage move two individuals—
a man and a woman, distinguished from one another
by gender, different in training, different in conditioning and expectations.

Man and woman. The natural complement of each
other. Two sexes flow through the yin and yang to
make a whole, a completeness, the union of two
complements in marriage. Man and woman seem to
be those two halves Plato told about that once having
been one creature Zeus then divided, who wander
the earth in search of their other half. "So ancient
is the desire of one another which is implanted in us,"
he says, "reuniting our original nature, making one of

two, and healing the state of man, that each of us when separated, having one side only, like a flat fish, is but the indenture of a man, and he is always looking for his other half."

It makes a beautiful scenario to see man and woman as parts of one whole. ". . . and the desire and the pursuit of the whole is called love." True, in part. The biological fit is an exquisite and procreative merging of our differences. And we *are* different, man from woman, husband from wife, mother from father, male from female, masculine from feminine.

Ideally, marriage goes beyond a meeting of complements into the realm of essences that have no sex, that transcend differences, realms of sharing those emotions and those qualities of self that are human and common to both of us. Marriage has always been the triumph of love and understanding over gender, and it always will be.

What happens, then, to prevent us from reaching that true sharing which occurs so rarely? Beyond the fact that no two human beings are ever totally compatible, part of the answer may lie in the roles assigned to us as men and women by culture and ancient traditions.

"The sex roles that men and women have filled have been functional and complementary," a psychologist has written. "If one is dominant the other is submissive; if one is active the other is passive; if one is independent the other is dependent; unemotional–emotional; insulated–expressive; silent–talkative; strong–weak; tall–short. This model of complementarity has served as the primary basis for male and female behavior in our society and the western world, if not [for] much of civilization."

It may be that complementarity is a workable model for a relationship, but as feminists and others have pointed out, women have traditionally been the negative half of the equation. Men are seen as doers, achievers, activators, protectors; women, as passive, expressive, the nurturing caretakers responsible for our emotional life in marriage. It is this kind of complementarity that sets men and women in different camps and effectively prevents them from becoming the full and complete persons they can be—in marriage, in any relationship. The theory of complementarity deprives each sex of the characteristics of the other; we are conditioned by it to believe that men and women want and need different things from life and from marriage.

When you get down to the heart of the matter, though, men and women really do want the same things out of marriage: a place to come home to; a sense of belonging; a place to love and be loved, need and be needed; the security in being known and accepted; and being able to count on someone for affectionate response, concern, and respect. Our perspective on the roles and needs of men and women have been altered now by the economic and technological changes of the last few decades and the questioning they generated; by the women's movement, the sexual revolution, and today's unprecedented emphasis on individual identity and fulfillment. We know that the old behavioral restrictions and definitions are not absolute and unalterable, yet men and women alike have been through a lot of hard knocks recently, trying to adjust to the new positions, new freedoms, new demands, while trying to hang on to something familiar and comforting from the old ways. It hasn't been easy.

As one man put it, "We know now that the old roles were terrible. We look back and say, 'My God, could we have been that wrong, that unjust, that hypocritical?' It has to change. But how, and where are we going? It has taken us a hundred years to begin to comprehend what racial equality means. How many more years do you think it will take to wash out the conditioning of thousands of years to reach women's equality, and change the way men and women think and feel?"

In the meantime, what do we do? Do we wait? Do we stop relating, waiting for the utopia of complete equality?

Some people, who are more role-bound than others, still gravitate toward marital relationships that will support the traditional ways of relating between men and women. If both partners agree that this is what they want, there will still be love and sharing, caring and loyalty. Any marriage that fulfills the needs of both husband and wife will work. Others, in increasing numbers, embrace the innovations of our society and adapt to new ways of relating that combine the old and the new. Very few women and men want to erase all the aspects of the old roles, all the attributes of masculinity and femininity. Neither men nor women want to give up the good and valuable qualities attached to old roles. What they *do* want is to add to their roles the good qualities each has been deprived of in the old order of things. Men want to be tender as well as strong and assertive, women want to be strong and assertive as well as tender. The thrust of the past decade's move toward equality has not been to make men and women exchange places or to take anything away from either, but to give each more of everything, to increase their repertoires and their range of emotions and capabilities as people, so that each can be more creative, more fulfilled.

But few of us really know how to handle these new expectations. The woman wants new freedoms, the man wants his old ones, and neither understands that they are not always talking about the same thing. There is enormous confusion, more conflict, more stress and distress than ever in relationships between men and women. In no place is it more evident than in marriage, because marriage *is* a structured relationship, a set of conditions and limitations and rules about our behavior, which has been seen as the last stronghold of the old role inequalities.

Even in the most traditional of today's marriages, however, the winds of change have had their effect. Everyone expects just a little more of marriage, and some expect a lot more. Resistant to change as marriage is, our expectations for it increase with each gain. We now expect to be companions, friends, partners, working and sharing equally in decision making, parenthood, in mundane household tasks, in responsibility, in sex.

There are couples who can successfully juggle the old and the new, who are not uncomfortable having old and new roles exist simultaneously in their marriages. They don't push for complete equality, but they won't accept a return to traditional and inequitable roles across the board. They remember that marriage satisfies their basic need for belonging, that it is a commitment to time and stability. They realize that changing to a different kind of marriage, to new responsibilities, to more equal roles, is only part of the foundation of their marriage. They know that caring, support, and empathy will carry them over the rough spots. These couples are achieving a new balance in their relationship, sometimes succeeding, sometimes failing. They are creating the new myths and ideals for men and women in marriage, partners in the struggle to be fulfilled human beings.

But it is a struggle. It is a difficult job to find a balance, and the burden of initiating change often falls on the woman. After all, men didn't ask for all the changes that have happened. They were happy with what they had—or at least thought they were. Since they didn't initiate the changes, they are the reactors, they are often on the defensive. For the most part, men liked their well-defined role as the producers, the bosses and decision makers in our society. Their identity did not depend upon their marriage or their woman. Their job and the outside world gave them an identity, and when the going got rough out there, the wife was waiting at home to soothe the bruises and bolster the ego.

To many men, the questioning and realignments going on today seem threatening, and the rewards uncertain. What do they stand to gain, what do they stand to lose? And who needs emotionality in a highly competitive world where those qualities get you nowhere? Men grew up expecting to be loved and cared for by Mommy, later to participate minimally in part-time fatherhood, to have real power where it counted and defer to the wife's power only at home, to have sex in marriage when it suited them and, better yet, to have sex outside when it suited them too. And now look what's happened. The man is expected to participate in full-time parenthood, to become housekeeper, shopper, secretary, baby-sitter, cook. Furthermore, everything he learned early in life about how to defend himself and conquer as a man—to be cool, uninvolved, masterful, and invulnerable—is now being held against him. He is asked to become more emotional, to be able to cry, talk about his feelings, communicate more expressively.

As the woman emerges into fullness, growing in strength, learning a new self-reliance, where is the man who is her companion? She needs him now as much as she ever did, but he may retreat into silence or sulking, or competing, retaliating, or playing power games. The woman yearns to get more of the emotional support she has always given to the man she loved, married to him or not, but the man, brought up to be competitive, not to show sensitivity, fearing to lose power, is often unable to give it to her.

"I think the basic problem in our marriage," one husband told me, "is that I am not able to express how I feel as much as Arlene would like me to express it. That's the biggest problem, to confirm what she probably knows is there. But I'm not an expressive person. So I have to learn to be more expressive about the way I feel toward her. And she has to try to recognize that it's difficult for me. We work on it, and I'm getting better, but it's hard if you never saw it in your own family."

It has been said, only half jokingly, that what the working woman needs now is a wife—someone to warm and comfort her after a long, hard day's work, someone to restore her and send her out refreshed, her ego bolstered. Having clean laundry and her clothes pressed would help too. It is no laughing matter. Each one of us in a relationship needs emotional nourishing. It's woman's turn now to get some of what she has always, and willingly, given in abundance to others. But she often finds that although she is growing into new responsibilities in areas that were once the man's province, men have trouble growing and expanding into the areas that were once exclusively hers.

As a family therapist points out, "Today both the man and the woman expect the other to be there for them, in a mothering, protective, nourishing way, in an enveloping availability, with open arms. Well, the traditional roles simply do not fit this mold."

Along with learning and adjusting to new roles, men have had to face up to their image as "symbols of oppression." Furthermore, even if they do change and grow in new directions, society still expects them to continue carrying out the responsibilities of their traditional roles. That view is now slowly beginning to shift, but by and large it is still embodied in our laws. To give them credit, many men have accepted in good grace this new version of the double standard, but it hasn't made things easier for them.

As one man, now in his forties, told me, "I've been through it all—my former marriage was built on all the old expectations, and when my wife wanted to be liberated, it didn't work. So then I divorced and I was free, but there was the bitter pill—I still had to support the kids. OK fine, I love them and want to support them and I have to, but there is always some argument over the fairness of it. Now I've remarried and it's entirely different. We both have jobs, and I think our marriage is fairly liberated. But I still have to support my kids. My point is that for all the liberation women are supposed to have, the economic pressure still remains on the man."

Other men rebel. They don't feel needed any longer, or they resent losing the image of themselves as macho strongman, adored daddy, final authority, the boy with the privilege of screwing around. Also, in this day of automation and anonymity, of big government, big business, big organizations of all kinds, many men find themselves trapped in boring or un-challenging jobs. They are cogs in huge machines and cannot satisfy their need for identity and importance in an increasingly impersonal world. So they must seek to satisfy those deep human needs in intimate personal relationships. Yet it is precisely here that men have been made to feel that they are lacking something. Is it any wonder that they feel all hands raised against them? That they wonder what they have left, where to turn? Who is to blame them? A man who feels trapped and inadequate in his marriage doesn't walk out of it, he runs. And he keeps running. He runs from relationships, from commitment, from responsibility.

The strong yet tender man, the loyal man, the understanding man who does try to change does exist, but he is not yet the stuff of which our heroes are made, at least not in the media. Machismo is still alive and well, the Marlboro Man still rides the range. We don't want to give up the image of the virile man but it is hard to believe in him when distorted concepts of masculinity are ever more loudly touted on our television screens, in films, in porno magazines, in all the raw sadism and violence we are subjected to. There are no new myths yet created for the humanistic man. Rollo May has said that myths are the inner, eternal truths that give meaning to our lives, give us our psychological and social identity. The strong, compassionate man is just beginning to emerge, but he is the anti-hero of books and films, not yet the stuff of which role models are made.

Society is still pushing men toward success in terms of position and material possessions. Liberation, self-awareness, expressiveness, more equal sharing in marriage and parenthood—these new demands are being incorporated into many marriages in many thoughtful ways. But most men are so busy trying to keep up with the old demands made on them that they have not yet begun to think in new terms. They are people trying to survive and enable their families to survive in an ever more pressured world. They are like Lou, who has been married to Theresa for twenty years and runs a successful restaurant.

Lou: My responsibility in marriage is the old-fashioned one to make sure my family is taken care of, money, shelter, their health. That's what a man's job is, even if he's got to stay away from home twenty-four hours a day to do it. And if the wife thinks he's getting a little on the side— well, as long as you bring home the paycheck, that's what's important.

Theresa: You'd better believe it—and I've had to give up a lot of time with my husband. Because of the kind of business he runs, sometimes it *is* twenty-four hours a day that he's gone.

Lou: I got a business to run and I like it. My customers call me Mr. Personality, and they know when I tell them to go to hell, it's my way of joking. Joking is how I keep healthy and sane. But the employees, they couldn't care less about this piece of equipment or that, and if you're not there to watch it, it's going to get costly.

Theresa: About twice a week I threaten that I'm going to go get a job. With four kids, we could sure use the extra money, and he might be home more.

Lou: But I won't allow my wife to work. While the children are young, they should have a mother. When they grow up, let her go to work fourteen hours a day.

Theresa: It's just a threat, though. For me the family is the important thing, and besides, I'm lazy, I don't want to work. I have enough to do at home. I don't think I could work all day and then come home and work more.

Lou: Watching the business the way I have to is where I sacrifice—by being away from my family. I get home sometimes for a few hours in the evening, to wipe my kids' asses if that's what's needed, but when I can't make it, there is no way in hell I got to be, like they say, a family man first. The business has to come first, or it goes under, and so do we.

Like many women, Theresa, too, understands the necessities of their life. Drastic changes in her lifestyle would not necessarily make either her or Lou happier. But for the women who want to step out of the old patterns, the push for long-deserved freedom and recognition has brought heartaches and headaches as well as advantages. In many cases, the pressures on women have increased enormously, and so have the conflicts, especially in marriage. The woman is expected to be all things—a career woman, a mother, a housewife, an emotional Band-Aid, an inventive and expert lover, an equal in mind and power. She is expected to be assertive, but still tender and feminine. She is expected to compete without being competitive. If she chooses to be a homemaker and mother, she is looked down upon by feminists and increasingly by men. She is expected to be able to juggle motherhood, career, and marriage, remain attractive, jog and exercise, pay her own way, open her own doors, and educate her man sexually and emotionally.

The battle for equality is still being fought; both men and women are becoming more aware every day of its confusion, alarms, and casualties. It is also, however, righting many injustices and clearing the way for new harmony and new forms of cooperation between men and women. Now that woman's position is changing, her options are increasing and her impatience is growing. She is moving into ever-expanding areas, developing more kinds of competence, learning to be more self-sufficient and assertive. Today women make up 40 percent of the labor force; 60 percent of all married women are working outside the home. Though most women still earn far less than men, more than two million women earn more than their husbands. Today, women do not have to marry, and they are taking advantage of that privilege in droves. With her life expectancy lengthened, a woman is spending only one-third of it in motherhood, and that only if she chooses and more and more she isn't choosing it. All this, plus contraception, education, and a changing sexual climate have expanded her vision of herself.

Everything adds up to a whole new set of expectations for women, in or out of marriage. Most women still want to marry, but today a woman asks what the price is, does it mean giving up what she's gained, will she be taken for granted? She expects to be treated as an equal, to be respected for her contributions, to share in decision making, to have some help with the housework, to have a career or job if she wants one, to enjoy sex for itself as a pleasure, to have the right to decide if she will have a child. She no longer wants to be a momma to her husband, at least not all the time. She wants a partner in marriage, a companion in life, a helpmate, a participant father. Most of all, she wants the emotional closeness and empathy she has always been called upon to give in a relationship. What she wants has added up to a whole new premise in marriage, different from her old one, different from his old one.

What do women want? was the big cry of the sixties, and we found that women wanted a lot more. As Dr. Estelle Ramey said at a recent conference, "It doesn't make any difference that Freud didn't know what a woman wanted. Every woman in this room knows what a woman wants—everything. Everything that's going. She may not be able to get it, but that's what a *man* wants."

It is a real dilemma that both men and women are facing today. It's new ground for both of them, and both are uneasy, testing, pushing, retreating, and questioning where it will lead them. There *is* a new balance in the relationships between men and women today, but we have no magic formulas to show us how to make it work. In theory, marriage is a fifty–fifty deal, and both partners have to put in a hundred percent of themselves. But the way it works out in reality, in the daily sharing of tasks, emotions, and problems, is a varying percentage—sometimes the balance will be 60/40, or 10/90. Sometimes he has more power, at other times she does. At any given moment, her needs may be greater than his, or vice versa. Much as we may aspire to and work toward equality in marriage, it is never exactly an equal arrangement. Only in time do the inequalities, the humanness of each, balance out.

Even our changing attitude toward sex roles does not mean instant alteration. It isn't that a door has been suddenly flung open; it is more like a stone cast into a pond where the ripples spread gradually in ever-widening circles. Two young working women talked about how they felt about the changes in roles.

Dottie: I think because women have changed, the men are changing, but they're finding it more difficult to adapt to all this.

Sandra: Because they don't have any background for it. They don't have anything to fall back on. They can't ask Dear Old Dad what he did, because the new man has to do something different. They can't do the same old thing.

Dottie: Dear Old Dad would probably lock Dear Old Mom in the closet until the problem blew over, but those Ozzie and Harriet things don't work anymore. The point we're at now is trying to get both men and women to adjust to each other, because this is new ground for both of us.

Sandra: We're in a period of transition, and by the time our kids grow up, we should see a big difference, the way our parents see a big difference in us.

Men and women are trying a little of this or that, both are finding that the new formulas are not any more "natural" to them than the old. The only thing that is natural is our humanness, transcending the roles of wife or husband, mother or father, protector or protected. Common to both, as a noted psychologist has said, are "tenderness, self-sacrifice, freedom to admit to fear and discomfort, forcefulness, independence, and willingness to expose oneself to change in order to live fully in the world—these are human qualities. . . ."

Men and women do speak a different emotional language, as one writer said, and "there's no one around to provide a simultaneous translation." But some are now beginning to listen together and to listen to each other. Neither wants to give up their inherent identities or the valuable sustaining qualities of their traditional roles. But they *are* making efforts to unscramble the codes and find a new balance in marriage.

13

The Home Front

There has been a lot happening on the housework
front, where compromise and working things out in
a marriage are often a question of two people not
wanting to do one dirty job—and that job has usually
been "woman's work," the kind my mother used to
say "is never done." On the behavioral level, we ar-
gue, we hurt, we are resentful, but many couples
finally do work things out and a lot of designs for
living are drawn up in the kitchen. Just one month
into their marriage, Lori and Ken had an argument
that is famous now in their family folklore.

Ken: The floor is dirty.

Lori: I don't think the floor is dirty.

Ken: I do.

Lori: Well, then, wash it.

Ken: But it's your job.

Lori: If it's my job, then I think the floor is clean.

Ken: But I think it's dirty, and I think it's your job to wash it.

Lori: I don't know how to wash a floor.

Ken: What did your mother teach you?

Lori: My mother did not teach me to wash floors.

Ken: But I don't like it the way it is.

Lori: Ah, not liking it is a whole different territory. If you don't like the way the floor is, that's a different problem. That's your problem. You can wash it or not wash it.

Ken: I don't want to do that, but I want it washed.

Lori: And I don't want to wash it. It would seem that a third person is necessary.

Recalling the argument some ten years later, Lori says, "Ken was in medical school at the time, and I was working. We earned about $4,800 a year, and out of that we managed to pay his full tuition, all our expenses, and Mrs. Whatever-her-name-was, who drank up all our liquor but did wash floors marvelously. So we've always had somebody like that, because the argument is a stupid argument."

When a wife and mother needs to work full time or wants a career, a whole other set of problems arises, and all the arrangements made up to then have to be redesigned, which does not mean that she loves her children less or is less concerned about their well-being or her husband's.

Some couples, like Suzanne and Martin, have been able to work it out better because they have help and because he is able to spend time with the children. They had married while he was still in law school, with all the old expectations for home and family.

Suzanne was a teacher, and couldn't wait to quit when they were expecting their first child. After that Suzanne went to the park, pushing a carriage, and did all the housework. "I had a fine time with that baby at home," Suzanne says. "She was a very good child, and it was easy to take off with one child wherever you wanted to go. With one child, I still considered myself a kid. We could pick up and go anywhere."

Three years later, their second child was born. "It was a weird feeling that suddenly came over me," Suzanne says. "I knew that with two children, it wasn't going to be that easy anymore. I knew right there in the hospital that I'd have to get a job. So I went home, and I was at home with both kids for seven months. I talked about getting a job, but you know how you talk about something and never do it. But I was finding that we'd go out to a party and I really didn't feel like talking to anybody because I had nothing to say. I didn't feel like talking about my children, I didn't feel like talking about what I cooked last night for dinner, and I decided that I had to do something about it right away. Martin and I figured out how much we could afford to spend on a housekeeper until I found a job, which I knew wasn't going to be easy. Especially since I knew I did not want to go back to teaching—I had two kids at home, and I didn't want to spend my working hours with more kids.

"Well, we figured that we could manage a housekeeper for two and a half months, and if I didn't find a job then, that was it. So I hired the housekeeper, and the next week, I had a job. We still have the same housekeeper after six years, and while she's not the greatest cleaner in the world, she's terrific with the kids, carts them around here and there, to school, lessons."

Martin says he has never thought of Suzanne in terms of a role as opposed to an individual. "The only thing I think of her doing that's a female thing is cooking, and that's because I don't like to cook. And she hates to clean, so our arrangement is that Suzanne cooks everything and I clean everything. There are men who think that's woman's work, but in our circle most of our friends all help."

The job Suzanne found moved her into the world of TV production, and she has risen steadily in the ranks of the organization. Today she earns more than her husband, which Martin sees as a benefit: "It would only bother me if it made Suzanne think less of me, which it doesn't."

"The hardest part of our life," Suzanne says, "and the only thing that keeps it on an even keel, is finding time to ourselves. We spend time with the children before and after dinner, but we try to have dinner alone. We have so much to say to each other at the end of the day."

"Years ago," Martin says, "I told Suzanne that I wanted her to work. It didn't have to do with finances, but I felt that working would make Suzanne a more well-rounded person. That was a little selfish, too. I thought it would make her more interesting for me. When she did go to work, it turned out I was not so happy about it at first because I didn't know how it was going to affect the kids, I didn't know how it was going to affect our relationship. But it was never a question of me 'letting' her work. Her mother used to say to me, 'How can you let Suzanne work?' Well, it's not my place to 'let'—she can do anything she pleases, she's her own person. She's not shackled."

"When I first went out to work," Suzanne says, "one friend thought I must be having a nervous breakdown. She told someone that I must be crazy because I was working, how could I leave my children? What may have done it for me was that I saw what my mother was like after my father died. I decided I was not going to turn out that way if it should happen to me. My mother was lost, she had never worked. She had financial security, but she had nothing to do with her time, and she still has nothing to do with it. I don't expect that my life is going to depend on what my children have in store for me twenty years from now. If they have kids, I'll be a nice grandma."

The tangle of roles, jobs, and parenthood that many couples face today isn't so easily resolved by everyone. Many, perhaps most, couples cannot afford to pay someone to clean; if there are young children and both partners are working, they can afford only daycare services. Perhaps all the money has to go to pay off the mortgage or to pay the children's tuition.

When there's no third party to do the housework, what does happen? Must the floors that need scrubbing, the laundry that has to be done, and the dishes piled up in the sink become the testing ground for the relationship? There can only be frustration, anger, and despair if the give-and-take accounts are reduced to that basis. I don't think there are any absolutes, that anything, even household work, can be divided exactly down the middle on a daily basis. But being fair is important, and there certainly needs to be a rebalancing today. In marriage, as in anything else, what we aim for is a balancing out in the end, a relationship where one person doesn't do all the giving and the other all the getting, one that aspires to equality but doesn't make petty or impossible demands.

But many women still meet a lot of resistance when it comes to sharing out a little more equally the tasks that are essential to keep a home working smoothly. Every study shows that working wives spend more hours in housework and have less leisure time than men. *Working Woman* magazine, for instance, reports that a working woman who spends the usual 35 to 40 hours a week at a paying job then does 41.1 additional hours of work a week caring for home and family. Women today, and men too, are making efforts to even out the load, not as a favor granted and a favor received, but as a fairer sharing.

Jane, who works full-time in publishing, found that equality on the home front involved a linguistic change—she and her husband found a new way to talk about dealing with their chores.

"At first," she says, "he would pitch in once in a great while, and then he would say peevishly, 'Why don't you thank me for helping?' So I would be properly grateful. After a while, I realized what was wrong and we had some arguments, and when he would fall back to his old position, I would say, 'Why don't you help with the cleaning?' He would say, 'Why don't you ask me to help?' Then I would say, 'It isn't for me to *ask*. The cleaning is there, it needs to be done. It's *our* house, not just mine, and it's our life and I'm working too.' It finally came down to revising the whole linguistic basis of it. He wasn't 'helping me.' We were both doing the housework. Now when I come home and he's waxed the floors, instead of saying, 'Thank you for waxing the floors,' I say, 'Gee, the floors look terrific.' Our big breakthrough was to realize that we were in this together, and to turn around the way we thought about it, we had to turn around the way we talked about it first."

We sometimes forget, though, that while some men are threatened by the changes in roles, so are some women. Although Jane cooks dinner, her husband and son pitch in and help in the cleanup. "Much as I needed it and wanted it," Jane admits, "I really had to deal in my own mind with having them take over the kitchen. It was like losing a part of me; the kitchen had been my territory completely for so long. Now it wasn't anymore. I had to come to terms with that. I had to give up caring where the cups were stored or how perfectly the dishes were washed."

"My husband lived alone for a good many years and managed to take care of himself," another young wife told me. "Yet he'd say something like, 'Is my green shirt ironed? No? OK, I'll do it.' I'd feel as though he were implying that I was a lousy wife because that damned shirt wasn't ironed. Well, it wasn't that at all. He didn't care, he knew how to iron a shirt. It was me—I had to get over the idea that there were fixed tasks for men and women."

The sharing can't be completely equal. Some men quite willingly wash the dishes and take on more responsibility in the household, as some men have always done. But they find that although their share of "woman's work" has increased, she isn't offering to do the plumbing or the electrical work, she doesn't wash the car or mow the lawn. When they live alone, women can learn very well how to do carpentry and repair jobs or to change washers, so there is some justice to the man's argument that the sharing of household tasks can mean his taking on her tasks, more than her taking on his.

Both men and women are seeing that women's new economic independence has had a real impact on roles both in the home and out of it. Money *is* power, and the woman's contribution to the family income does give her a strong lever for changing the balance in the domestic part of the relationship. "It was really hard," Lori says, "early in our marriage, when I was working full time and he was going to school. When I came home he wanted me to get dinner, he had exams to study for. I said there will always be exams to study for. He had to learn to contribute. The person—me, in this case—earning the money had some rights in terms of what was expected from the homebody. When the fights really got bitter, we compromised and went out for a pizza."

Later on, when Ken was out of school and working, and Lori worked only part time, things changed. "When I had a little job and Ken had two big ones, it occurred to me that if I didn't do something in terms of cooking, you know, home stuff, then I was a bad investment. It's always been in the back of my mind that I do have some responsibility to do something, that marriage isn't a free trip. And it really does come down to money in a way. If I'm not earning a salary, then I have to do more stuff at home.

"Right now, I see the children as being my main job, and they get me off the hook. We both feel that that's all right, that I am pulling my fair weight, I'm doing my job. When the girls are older, I plan to go back to work, that's why I spent those years getting a degree before we had children. And now that we have them, they're a big financial responsibility. We've decided that where I can get a job is more important than where he can get a job. As a doctor, he's employable wherever we go, but there are only a few college towns where I am employable at all. If we relocated we would pick a place that I could go with my head, not only as a wife."

Responsibilities and tasks shift back and forth, but for those couples who know that the home-front exchange is only one aspect of their relationship, and not the crucial one, all kinds of arrangements can be made and changed to suit the needs of the moment, the demands of jobs, the likes and dislikes of each partner. For Vince and Leah, for instance, a reversal of the usual household areas suits them just fine—not because of liberation or rights or power, but simply because of their personalities. He's neat and orderly and enjoys cleaning. She's not. She hates to clean, but likes keeping accounts. They've worked it out so both do what best suits them. For Dee and Bob, things are more traditional. Although she works, she still does most of the household work, because "It gives me a lot of satisfaction, putting things in order. He'll pitch in when I ask him to, but it's no big problem for us."

Julie, the mother of two children who are now ten and twelve, was an editor before her marriage and worked at home on a free-lance basis while her children were small. She recently began working again full time in the administration of a large New England college. "Everyone has a job, sort of, in marriage," she says, "and my husband and I are now adjusting or readjusting ours. It's sort of a lateral movement on both our parts. He was polarized in the job area, and although I never stopped working, I felt polarized in the home area. Now we're both moving, so that he is embracing more of the home. I've let go of the home much more and am centering myself on the job. Speaking very, very practically, I contribute to our income, which translates, I hope, into relieving him of some of the pressure of things like paying off the mortgage and educating the children. And I hope it will make him live longer. I may get the ulcer instead as I get more into the emotional stress of my work, but that's the way it is."

To be sure, some men still have mixed feelings about their wives working, and from time to time those feelings surface. Many women, like Harriet, are encouraged by their husbands to work full time if they want to—up to a certain point, that is. "He encourages me in every way, except when we have an argument. And then the first thing he throws up in my face is, if you weren't working, we would have such and such, and he goes down a whole long list of complaints—the house would be clean, the kids would be better behaved, we would get this or that activity done. He says he enjoys my working, but it seems that if the first thing he mentions in an argument is my working, then he's not terribly pleased. But I have to get out of the house. My job is vital to me and so is my marriage, so we manage to work it out."

Sometimes it just doesn't work out. There may be too many gaps in the relationship, too many conflicting aspirations and expectations, too many points on which there can be no agreement. Lynn's marriage is an example. I first met Lynn when she interviewed us during a promotional tour for one of our books. She was intelligent, articulate, self-assured. We corresponded over the years and met again recently. Lynn said she was going through a process of formulating the future, conceiving her goals and figuring out how to attain them. A career in television has always been her life's desire, but, as she said, "You don't just bounce into New York and say, 'I want to be at Barbara Walters' desk right now.'" Besides local interviewing, she had worked on the development of a videotape program for the city school system.

Lynn had told me that she had had many chances to marry, but none of the men had conquered her deep-down reluctance to "put the brakes on a lot of things that I liked doing." Then she met and married a man she loved and admired. They now have a two-year-old child.

I was taken aback when she told me that the marriage was far from happy. "The sad thing is that just what I expected happened," she explained. "He started to put on the brakes. He chased me so hard, and he said he married me because he thought I was interesting. Then his true expectations started to come out: 'Now you are married, you have got to clean the house. Why haven't you done it?' And all the things we ever had in courtship started going out the window, plus the awful fights that I never realized could be so brutal. He's rather cruel about it, too. In trying to push me into the mold, he uses everything from berating to physical force. I never realized that when you get married, there are no holds, no rules. It's nice for the court to say you can't do this or that, but when you are in an apartment or home and the doors are closed to the outside world, there are no rules. I know exactly what is wrong with my marriage, but I don't know how to make it right."

Lynn describes her husband as a man of forceful personality, very successful in his business, very smart. "But he's a yeller and screamer, and I'm not. I'm the type who builds up motivation and then I act on it. If I have to, I'll say goodbye, very cleanly, without too many tears. He'll yell and scream and try to get his way, like a little child. He's the closed-marriage type, and he knows it's wrong, but he can't seem to help himself."

When her husband was transferred out of town for a while, they managed somewhat better in a part-time marriage, but now he is back and she feels that his attitude is not only constricting her but is causing problems for their child. "It was hard for me because I was determined that I was going to have a career. I always loved the outside world and dealing with ideas and people. I still haven't made a great success of myself but an unhappy marriage isn't helping. It's very damaging, in fact. I can see where women are very damaged by marriage if it isn't working out and they don't have a helpful husband. I really don't want to be the kind of person he wants me to be, I really don't want to be just a housewife.

"The mother part, though, I really like. I see some purpose in it, and I really enjoy it. The thing on my mind now is not to let my child be affected by the pressure in my marriage. That, and trying to solve economic problems, are my two largest goals. I'm actually putting the marriage aside for a little bit because I am so concerned about those two things. If the marriage goes, I still have these two things, my child and my work, but somehow it won't work in reverse. I'm afraid that if I take my energy from the other things and put it into marriage and if that fails, then there will be zero.

"He feels that I can't work on my career at the same time as I have children. The real problem is that he feels left out. When we had counseling—which didn't really work out—our therapist said it's the relationship he had with his mother, which is based on the biological tie, not on intimacy. He never had a real mother-and-son spiritual bond, and it's hard for him to get close to a woman from an intimate point of view. He hasn't seen his mother more than once in five years. I want to keep in touch with my parents. We're close. But my husband doesn't understand. He wants me to be devoted to him and to take care of him; that's my prime duty in life. He wants me to do all the same things his mother did for him, and all the rest, too. And sex hasn't been that terrific either. It's hard for him to get in touch personally. He can deal more with things, machines.

"He just doesn't understand the intimate, the emotional. That's one thing, and the second is that he feels my work must be valueless, because it doesn't have a formal time structure, like a nine-to-five secretarial job, and especially since I'm not making much money. He says, 'You're just fooling around, wasting your time. Get home and make the food.' That's his attitude."

In Lynn's marriage, the full force of conflict between the old and new roles, the disparateness between woman's new expectations and aspirations and man's old ones were painfully visible. Motherhood, work, domestic roles—every area where women are trying to make adjustments and find new ways of fulfilling their obligations and new ways of fulfilling themselves—these are the battlefields where Lynn found herself every day. And the battles were bitter, for real. There was little fun in trying to make it work. The basic premises Lynn and her husband have about marriage and their goals are entirely different. Unless one or the other changes, how can it work, in terms of today's world?

"I have moved out," she wrote me recently, "for all the reasons I told you about, me, our child, the discouragement, my career, all of it. It seemed to me the only solution. We're trying to work it out on a part-time basis."

Other couples have managed to make choices that satisfy both the man and the woman, as we have seen. Many women prefer being full-time homemakers and mothers, but more and more they keep their options open, do not tie themselves down absolutely to their motherhood function. Connie made sure she knew what she wanted to do before having children, so that she could return to working when they were old enough. Even now, though, she spends as much time as she can studying and pursuing other activities. "The worst trap I see a lot of my friends getting into," she says, "is I Have to Be the Mother for That Child, Who Can Do It Better Than Me? Well, nobody, but you'd better start learning, because when will there be that magic day when you can let somebody else take care of your kids?

"A lot of people sort of pick at me and say, 'Don't you feel you use too many baby-sitters?' My mother used to go off and write, and we had sitters, and I always knew that when my mother came home, she wanted to see us. I'm sure now that she spent more time with us than she wanted to and it loused up her writing life, but I didn't realize it then. I was always proud that my mother had something better to do than make tuna fish. It always bothered me when my friends' mothers didn't have anything they wanted to do. Whether or not my mother was writing, my mother was a writer.

"One of our friends said, 'I never knew couples where both did something and had children too.' And I answered, 'That's not a good reason not to have children. You don't *want* to have children is a terrific reason, but not because you don't think you can handle your career and being a mother.' I have one friend who has a very satisfying and demanding job, and is now on maternity leave for her first child. I asked her if she's really going back to work the middle of next month. She said, 'Oh, sure.' And I said, 'No, really, are you going to do it?' She finally said, 'I don't know.'

"I said, 'It's fun having a kid, isn't it? Well, we did try to warn you that the real reason people don't go back to work is not because they're trapped at home, but because it's really fun. It beats working.' "

Many young women do manage both children and a career, some, of course, better and with less difficulty than others. In the past, women had careers too, after all, though not as many as today. Fortunately, some of the problems working mothers have can be solved more easily today because of our greater economic and job mobility, allowing more and more women to interrupt careers or a job when they want to have children. I talked with one who was planning her life this way.

"I really believe in the theory of cycling your life," she said. "There are years when it's appropriate to be available to youngsters, and there are years when it's appropriate to be very busy with your own life and doing meaningful work in the world. My career is in second place now. In a few years, it won't be. I know the anxieties women have who are home, some of them facing emptiness and depression. They wonder if being home raising children now means being nowhere at forty. It's not easy when you go to a dinner party and other people, even the women, no longer respect your being a housewife and mother. 'What *else* do you do?' they ask. Women want more and they should have it, but there are other considerations.

"What I am against is the idea of throwing up your life in a day and changing the whole set of ground rules overnight. Suddenly life is no longer ordered or meaningful; it's chaos. If you are going to leave home and go out to work or go to law school, there has to be some preparation and education and evolution within the family and the marriage. You and the children and your husband grow into it. You don't make pawns of your children or your husband or yourself. I've seen women taking jobs outside the home when I'm not convinced that they really want them, without any great sense of the future or the job. Many women are sitting behind desks doing the dumbest work in the world in exchange for raising a family."

In the changes we see taking place on the home front, the area of parenthood seems to be one where the most significant gains are being made—perhaps, among other things, because, unlike an unwashed dish or the laundry, children give pleasure along with problems. For all the tedious parts of child raising and the time it takes, the benefits are tangible and immediate. Fathers are finding that taking a greater share in parenting brings immense rewards. When I first met Valerie and Richard on a summer weekend several years ago, I was impressed by their devotion and the ease with which they seemed to be carrying out all the new ideals. She was a lanky young mother in blue jeans, working for a graduate degree; he was an affable guy just starting in business. Richard was carrying their new baby around in a harness on his back. They were both so earnest about the future, and I thought they were starting out easily and delightfully in sharing parenthood.

Half a dozen years later the baby on his father's back was an active, bright youngster and there was a second baby sitting on his father's lap. What had seemed so easy to me turned out not to have been that simple. Richard recounted what had happened.

"I entered fatherhood in a very, very old-fashioned way," he said, "which created absolutely horrendous fights between us. The fundamental problem was that I grew up in a home where my mother serviced my father, and my father didn't do a damn thing around the house. So my model was one of non-involvement when Peter was born. Valerie and I had some pretty brutal, knock-down, drag-out bouts over diapering and things of that sort. I felt put-upon as no man has ever felt put-upon. And I can tell you, I thank my lucky stars that I married Valerie and that she took the attitude that she did, because I know I never would have gotten into the kids the way I did or enjoyed them the way I do.

"I haven't any hesitation now; we share those responsibilities now. And hell, yes, I still feel put-upon sometimes. I come home from the office and have had a lousy day and just want to sleep, and at three o'clock in the morning, Valerie says, 'Hey, the pipsqueak is yelling and it's your turn'—well, I don't engage in a battle anymore because basically there's something that emerges between me and Pipsqueak at three o'clock that's awfully nice. I have a real feeling of attachment to these kids that I have to lay at the doorstep of this change in me. And yet, my relationship with the kids recognizes our differences, and the things I enjoy doing with them and those I do not.

"I don't really get turned on reading Peter stories; I felt very quickly after I got into it that that was cheating him. A child can sense that. So we do other things. I really look forward to making breakfast on weekends when he helps me. Peter will tell you gratuitously that *he* makes the best omelets in the house, which makes Daddy puff out this far. And this sense of closeness, this personal feeling and enjoyment, is an outgrowth of some of the fights Valerie and I had early on over how we were going to bring up these kids. And they weren't things we talked about at all before we got married or even before we had children. It was really Valerie and her attitude about sharing our roles that set the thing going straight."

If Richard discovered the joys of parenthood the hard way, the results can be just as rewarding when participatory parenthood is accepted and planned for ahead of time. Jeff is a writer and so is his wife, Carrie, and both believe in greater equality between men and women. He knew he wanted to be a big part of their daughter's life. His time with her on walks, in the city and the country, at breakfast, while caring for her, taught him things about life he had never examined before. "Caring for a child means developing long-suppressed abilities to see—really see—another human being. It means comforting her, laughing with her, preventing her from doing herself harm, and learning how to express emotions in the most honest way possible. There is no way, for example, not to recognize the undisguised joy or pain or confusion of a three-year-old child."

In an article he wrote about learning from his child, he said that "being with my daughter has taught me something about what it means to be open with another human being. It seems to me that the objections to male 'armoring' is one of the most perceptive aspects of the feminist argument, and I've come to believe that one of the most hopeful ways to increase honesty between husbands and wives is to have actively participating fathers."

It simply isn't possible, of course, in many cases, for fathers to participate fully in the daily lives of children. As Lou said earlier, "The business has to come first, or we go under." The demands of Ken's work as a doctor keep him away from his wife and children for days on end. "Ken is very good and he's very conscientious about his work, but he'd rather see me and the kids for breakfast than make rounds at seven," Lori says. "He has no choice about that sort of thing, but he hates the fact that he can't be there with us."

Even with all these problems, compared with their counterparts of a few decades ago, these couples have gone a long way toward complete sharing. One woman, who has been married for twenty-nine years and today has a good marriage, for instance, now admits her mistake of having tried to take on all the burdens singlehanded.

"I realized after eight or ten years of marriage that I had made all the mistakes," she says. "I was a demon running around and having the kids pick up all their toys so that the house was neat and clean when

Daddy came home. So dear Daddy didn't have to share too much in the mess and the problems. I think that was probably my greatest mistake as far as our marriage is concerned. I protected him too much from the disorder and clutter he hates. As a consequence, he never realized what I had to contend with all day long. The tension in the air was so thick you could cut it with a knife, because 'Daddy's had a long, hard day at the office.' But this was the way I was raised, 'Daddy this, and Daddy that,' and we must all be on our best behavior when he comes home. Best behavior, hell. It was the end of my day and it was the end of the children's day, too, and we were all tense. But I tried to protect him, and sometimes we would all end up in a screaming match to protect Daddy, and it didn't do a bit of good. I should have let him walk in on the mess of toys. I should have said, 'You take over now while I get dinner.' I made a mistake, I really did, but how did I know any better?"

No matter when you were married, what can make it work better today is the agreement factor, mutual understanding and agreeing upon the responsibilities involved in living together, in raising children, in choosing roles. Ben and Kitty, in more than twenty years of marriage, have weathered numerous changes in their roles and in their responsibilities to each other and to their children.

"The responsibility thing," says Ben, "is a very shifty one in some families, at least in ours, because there has been an almost total reversal of responsibilities. We had a very traditional type of relationship, aside from the fact that Kitty was very much ahead of her time in many ways—she was working, for one thing, right from the beginning. She still looked to me for the kind of traditional responsibilities men had when we were first married. Over the years, and especially since I started working free-lance at home,

I began to take on a lot of the responsibilities that are supposed to be a woman's, and more so now that Kitty has landed a very important and demanding job. I begin to see a lot of the things that I had no way of comprehending, like what's involved with the emotional pull a child has on the parent who's at home. I think a father who's not at home really doesn't know, can't ever understand it. It's all very well for your kids to know that they can call you or come to you if there's a problem; that's positive. But for the person there full time, there's a tremendous pull.

"I like to go to my typewriter and work and not be disturbed, but if one of the kids is at home and needs something, you have to respond. When I talked about it to Kitty, she said, 'I had that for years,' and I began to understand what a lot of women are talking about. The responsibility gets to be the thing that has to be done, by whoever is there to do it. And if you're going to think in a traditional way, it's going to be a real problem. It's always worked out for us because we never really gave a damn about what anybody else thought. We were strong within ourselves because we had each other for support. If we hadn't, we couldn't have made it, and it's made us even stronger."

This mutual support can exist with or without radical role changes. Sylvia and Gordon have come through thirty years of marriage without feeling they needed to be liberated. Now that their children are on their own, Sylvia has become an interior decorator, an outgrowth of her hobby of painting, but she is not about to become a totally liberated woman or change her role in her marriage. "When you're playing the game of man versus woman, or woman versus man, which it has become lately," she says, "you have to be very careful about the roles. Roles are very important. Femininity is very important, and I enjoy my role.

Whatever has happened in our life, and we've certainly gone up and down, we've weathered the storm pretty well just by being the two people we are."

The point is, of course, that marriages are defined by the partners involved, and they are as good, happy, or successful as the partners feel about them, no matter what role changes occur or are considered and rejected. Change is an option, and there are many ways of finding a balance that fits. Many couples, for example, are not as affected as others by the new demands and role changes. They hear of them, and consider them in the light of their own marriages.

I know that for myself, my choices and my husband's have led us on a path that is quite different from the one my parents had. I was the maverick in the family anyhow, the first one to go to college, the first to leave home, the first to go to a larger city. And I married someone completely foreign to our family's midwestern background. But, then, there was always a strong streak of independence in my family. Hadn't Mother and Dad been pioneers in their own way, setting out from the plows and farmlands their ancestors had pioneered to survive alone in a big city, a new environment requiring new skills and new ways of adapting? Long before the early feminists, my aunts had left the farm for the city, not for marriage, but to work in offices and factories. They chose marriage and a family later, to be sure, just as my mother chose to work before the family became her full-time occupation. And in the light of today's views on child raising, for our time, my brothers and I had a non-sexist upbringing. My father taught me to drive at the age of twelve, expected me to help paint the house, do carpentry, fix the car, and know how to wire a lamp. My brothers both learned to cook, wash dishes, and iron their own clothes. We all pitched in, sharing the tasks as needed.

Although my father worked outside the home he was as integral to our parenting as Mother was. They were both equally the hub of our world. Rooted and routine as their life seemed, I realize that my love of travel, of seeing the new, must also come from them. We tootled around in old Fords and Chevys to anything worth seeing within reasonable distance, to the Capitol in Washington and the Smithsonian Institution, to Niagara Falls, the World's Fair in Chicago, the snake mounds in Ohio, the foliage in the fall. We were forever piling into and out of those unheated cars to visit family, steaming through the snowdrifts in the mountains to share Christmas on the farm. Yes, we were family-oriented and children-oriented, with happy memories now that my brothers and I have built our own families and lived through long marriages of our own.

It is interesting to see how the three of us have gone our different ways in marriage from the same roots. My brothers are even more family-oriented than my parents, than I am, one with four children, the other with five. My young brother, Jerry, followed in our father's footsteps, working for the same company, and he married Joanne, a local girl, generous and easy-going. My older brother, David, married Ann, a southern girl, and settled in Georgia, where he is a dentist and also teaches at the university.

They are both happy in their marriages, happy with the activities of their children, with their own occupations. They are good fathers, work around the household, and are enthusiastic about their family and their home. David helped Ann with the diapering and burping of their five children while he was working and going to dentistry school at the same time. They have gone through privations to earn their comfort and success. Ann enjoys running her large home that is always overflowing with kids, friends, neighbors, and family. Jerry's wife, Joanne, is both a homemaker and a full-time working woman, and has been since the first day of her marriage with four children now nearly grown. I am struck, when I see them now, with how little their roles have to do with the way they feel about their marriages. Identity is never a question with them.

Both couples, I know, have been through rough periods, of needing confirmation, of wanting something more or different, of struggling with the actions of love, but they have never phrased these dissatisfactions or longings in terms of "finding myself." This question may come later, as it often does, in mid-life, but so far they have never articulated their problems in terms of "Who am I, what am I, where am I going?" Their marriages have withstood the periods of apartness, of doubt and anger, rejection, all the things everyone feels at some time in a long-term relationship, but they seem to work it out pretty fairly. Each seems to have an ingrained sense of fairness, a grounded sense of self.

Since Joanne works, she and Jerry share more equally on the home front. They have their separate nights out. Oh, yes, they questioned a little each other's "rights and duties" at the height of the women's movement, but then they looked at themselves and decided that what they had was a good arrangement, and no one was going to tell them what was fair or wasn't. They adapt their roles to the needs of the moment. There were raised bayonets for a while over the fact that he took his golfing and hunting vacations each year and she never took a vacation alone. But he said, "I never said you shouldn't go. You've been talking about going to New York for eighteen years, but you never do it." And Joanne, realizing that she, not he, had held herself back, now buzzes off on trips to visit us in New York or to see other friends.

Neither of them for a moment has expressed the need to search for self; they *know* who they are, they know what suits them. And if they have felt at moments the need for more affection, have at times been distant and dissatisfied, they hammered it out. The bond between them grows stronger and is reinforced when some family emergency arises or they meet some personal crisis. They are good, solid people for whom marriage has the meaning of constancy—but they are not unaware of their options. They know divorce is possible, and have even said that they could very well exist independently, but they prefer to be together. In both my brothers' families, now that the heavy going of making their place in life is over and their children are growing up, I see a new kind of romance between them, a closeness that was submerged in the bustle of their earlier years. They have what I think are good marriages.

In discussing the changes in marriage today, the couples I have talked with consistently mention the same two things that make the most difference between making it and not making it in a marriage— choice and agreement. Whether the foundations stand as a solid base for marriage, whether the couple can hold together through all the new rough periods and new pressures, whether they can build or rebuild the House of Marriage they create together depends on their feeling of having chosen what they want, on having done it and being able to redo it. You can make a whole catalog of the ingredients of a good marriage: admiration, respect, good communication, trust, privacy, flexibility, understanding, empathy, intimacy, identity, loyalty. But even all of them together won't make the marriage successful unless there is an agreement, tacit or voiced, by both partners about what their premise is—what they want and what their values are. And even then, with all these qualities we know can work for our benefit, it's still tough.

As one young woman put it, "It's a very complex life most of us are involved in. It's a very hard thing to live life, and the more we take on ourselves, the more conscious we have to become about what our priorities are. If you don't order them, they will order themselves—and maybe in a way you don't want. I value roots and meaningfulness in my family, in myself, in us. Values are very abstract unless you make them real. And it takes doing to make them real, make them happen."

We create ourselves by our choices; we create our marriages by our choices, and the priorities we place on certain aspects of our lives. On the one hand, choices *are* limiting—if we choose one person or life-style, we automatically rule out others. On the other hand, these choices free us to explore other dimensions of our lives, to be flexible within the commitment of marriage, the kind of marriage we choose. One man told me, "What really holds our marriage together is our mutually agreed upon values and how we live them. If my wife weren't with me on these values, then we wouldn't have a real marriage."

In the past, many decisions about roles, work, and parenthood didn't have to be made. We knew what our values were, our marriages were all cut from the same piece of cloth, and there was usually agreement. The changes in society today force us to decide, either to change or remain where we are, to hang on to old values or create new ones. Today people in marriage need to focus more sharply on what they want and can agree to. By having some central core of agreement on their premise in marriage, couples can more easily meet the inevitable changes to come.

14

What's Happened to Sex in Marriage?

Sex is a deep instinctive drive, a universal component of the marital relationship, and as it happens, a preoccupation of the time in which we live. We think about sex, talk about it, are reminded of it wherever we look. We seek new ways of experiencing it, try to make it better for ourselves, but whatever we do with it, it is there, a powerful physical drive, a biological force that colors our attitudes, our roles, our lives. We try to understand and come to terms with it. And today more than ever we are concerned with the place of sex in marriage.

Pat, who has been married for three years and is about to have her first baby, told me recently, "I thought sex after you got married had to be boring because everyone that's married seems to be going around with this great obsession about sex—in their bed, in someone else's bed. I thought something must happen that made it really bad after you got married. How could it be so different from all the affairs I've had? Well, I was very surprised that I haven't found that to be the case. Maybe if you're married twenty years, it's different, but it is still great for us. Happily, we know that married couples in every age group are having more sex today than ever before."

But if Pat is expressing doubt about marital sex, is it any wonder, what with everything that has been happening on the sexual scene in the past ten years? Inhibitions are out, sexual freedom and expectations for bigger and better and different sex are in. We have been delivered a barrage of information and misinformation about sex unprecedented in the annals of any society. Sex is everywhere, and what we hear and see of it tends to confuse as much as it educates us. In the process, the difference between the genital orientation of the sex huckstered and merchandised by the media and marital sex embedded in a relationship of love and commitment is often forgotten. Somehow the caring, the empathy, and the special meaning of sex in marriage is lost. Some couples do recognize the difference and know what it is that satisfies them; they can take the national preoccupation with perpetual orgasm in stride.

Expressing how married sex means something different from what she sees of sex outside of marriage, Andrea says, "I'm a very physical person, and I realize that maybe part of the reason my husband and I chose each other was that we have about the same level of need. He needs a lot of hugging and I need a lot of kissing, and so it works out pretty well.

It isn't 'Gee, we haven't had sex in such and such amount of time.' It just sort of happens.

"It wasn't like that when I was dating, when you had to rush it because a date lasts only just so long. I'm happier this way. A lot of my single friends come in with these cock-and-bull stories about sex, six hours in bed and nine million affairs. With my husband, I just don't think of it in those same terms." Sex in marriage is different; it's making love, lovemaking, powerful, mysterious, the flow of union and communion, and having pleasure and fun. But today, one wonders if that's enough.

Delores, who's been married a few years longer than Andrea, puts it this way: "It's occurred to me in passing, with various people I've met before and after I got married, that maybe I could have had a very thrilling sexual experience with them. It's sort of something you note—different time, different place. With all the things you see and read, though, I sometimes feel we're out of the mainstream because we're not sexually daring. And then I think that that doesn't matter very much. Being married is more important."

Not everyone is as levelheaded as Andrea and Delores, though, in the face of the sex explosion of recent years. The peculiarly American obsession with sex and the exploitation of it have affected almost everyone to some degree or another. Witness Delores's feeling that, despite her good relationship with her husband, perhaps they are out of the mainstream, because they aren't "daring." Our national preoccupation with sex has moved into the marital bedroom along with all the changes in roles, and it isn't easy to put sex in its proper perspective in our lives.

No one denies, least of all me, that we needed some loosening up in the holier-than-thou attitude we Americans have long had toward sex. But how much have we really been loosened up, and what are the real gains from the sexual revolution for men and women and marriage? We are learning more about sex. We know that sex is for pleasure as well as procreation and that both men and women have the capacity for and the right to sexual fulfillment. We now have a wealth of new and valuable information about sexual functioning and our sexuality. But the knowledge we have gained has come to us colored by several important factors: our decade's emphasis on self-involvement, confusing changes in our sex roles, and the media explosion.

The excellent and responsible coverage of sex in magazines, in newspapers, and on television is for many people the main source of education and information about sex. For all their inestimable value, the media do tend to exaggerate or otherwise distort information. What has resulted is not only a demystification of sex but a tendency to wrench it out of context and set it apart as a topic, an exhibit, a function in and of itself. But we don't, in marriage, make love in a vacuum, in an isolated bed. Sex in marriage is not just a physical act of the moment, but one to which we bring our past, present, and future.

Much of the focus of the sexual revolution has been on the genital and mechanical aspects of sex. It's his orgasm, her orgasm, kinds, size, frequency, gadgets, aids, creams. Sex has been depicted, analyzed, diagramed, programed, and therapized out of any innate eroticism it may have. Sex has been merchandized and sold like detergent or new cars; it is the ideal product for our consumer society—what more lucrative need to pander to than one that is a basic drive, one in which men and women are vulnerable, needful, and, as the huckster would say, so turned on by. The result? New desires created, old needs revved up, new dissatisfactions, new frustrations, and new —perhaps impossible—expectations for both sexes. The saturation is complete, from books on sexual techniques to sex therapy clinics, from articles and lectures to the array of magazines at the corner newsstand and the programs we see on television, all of it reminding us of needs we should have, instructing us on how to be fulfilled, and making us all wonder if we are missing the latest things. Are we keeping up with the Joneses in their bedroom?

No one anymore can rest easy about his or her sexual relationships. As one man said, "It's got to be such a focal point, everyone is reading all these books. If your sex life isn't satisfactory, they say, try this, try that, try this. It got so that I felt like I was back in college. I was reading textbooks in a college course, grade level one. And that just has to be funny when it comes to something like sex."

But it isn't so funny. Not when some people end up feeling like efficiency experts, not when they become robots who are technically proficient, but emotionally deficient. Not when, after reading and seeing and hearing about what you should be doing, you find you aren't, you can't, or you won't, and you end up wondering what's wrong with you. The new information about sex, our mechanical aids and pornographic stimulations, our pilgrimages to sex clinics, have not turned out to be the panaceas or instant aphrodisiacs they were thought to be because what has been overlooked is the meaning of sex in the context of a relationship.

Even the most solid couples can be affected by what's in the air. Rick and Barbara have been married for half a dozen years. They have two children and are knowledgeable, articulate people who know what they want out of their life together. It never really occurred to me when I interviewed them that they could have been affected, with all their possession of the critical faculties and their ability to withstand the blandishments of the media.

Rick said, "We see so little of the sexual revolution in our daily round of life. We are primarily family oriented, have a nice group of friends who are pretty much like us. But I think there's a tendency to put a premium not just on sexual compatibility, how you make it in bed, but also on the frequency of sex. You think there must be something wrong with you if you are not flipping into bed with each other every night. And no one tells you that, when you've got kids and are busy in your business life, you might not be up to having sex with any frequency. Not even if Raquel Welch walked in the door. It has nothing to do with how much in love you are with your wife. How comfortable you are is the important thing. Yet when you're under a lot of pressure and tension, one of the truly wonderful things is climbing into bed and just holding each other."

I thought, how realistic. These people have their feet on the ground. Then Barbara piped in with, "But somehow, it's shaky. 'Wait a second,' you say. 'Is there something wrong here, something wrong with us?' We look at our emotional relationship and know there's nothing wrong. Then why is it we aren't turning on to each other five times a week instead of two? It's very easy in the climate to lose sight of the good and the important reasons and go back to the statistics in the current issue of some popular magazine. And all this discussion in the media about sex therapy and frequency statistics increases anxiety. How can it *decrease* anxiety because the first thing you think about is, 'Am I up to the magazine statistics?' And you ain't right unless you've got everything going for you every day of the week and twice on Sunday."

The pressure on married couples is, as Barbara notes, not only on frequency but on performance as well. And performance is associated with our roles as men and women. Each partner is urged on to ever greater delights in sex. Can she have multiple orgasms? Can he? Can they both satisfy each other and themselves, and how? Both expect more of each other and themselves. Today there are ways of making comparisons. A man watches a pornographic film and compares his performance with that of the studs, not stopping to realize that it may have taken four days and numerous rest periods for that glorious erection to last through one sexual act on film. The woman also compares herself to others, and wonders where she's at if she doesn't measure up.

Debbie, with two children and a marriage of seven years, says, "I have a friend who called me up and said, 'I can't have orgasms anymore. What should I do?' She's asking me? Who knows beans? What do I know? So we got to talking about it, and I got to reading up on it, and now I'm not sure I ever had an orgasm."

Debbie may well have had an orgasm, but she may never have experienced exactly the kind the descriptions tell her about, a blast like 10 on the Richter scale. Now she may doubt even what she does have, or did have. Besides, descriptions of orgasm seldom mention all the ingredients that go into making it an earth-shaking blast. Certainly we have needed to have more information about sex to counteract the puritanism and the hiddenness of sex which have deprived us of fully knowing and enjoying the sensuality of our bodies and experiencing the completeness of uninhibited passion in sex. Certainly we needed to divest sex of its idealism and enjoy it for the earthy, delicious experience it can be. But aren't we now asking sex to accomplish a different kind of impossibility? What we need now, above all, is a way to put together all the new information we have and integrate it with our hearts and feelings as well as our bodies, to show how it works in *relationships.*

We are urged to be more communicative with each other in our sexual activities—to tell each other in the closeness and intimacy of sex what we need and want. But how much openness can we have about an area as delicate as sex if we haven't learned to be open and to communicate honestly with each other about anything else? Many couples are still uneasy when it comes to talking about their own sex, in bed and out of it. The man resents being told, the woman is still reluctant to express what she wants. It requires a shift in roles, just as in the other areas of our lives, to become more open and intimate.

Our conditioning in sex roles is even more of an impediment to understanding each other in sex than in other areas, and the resultant misunderstandings are more massive and more painful. Although we know now from tons of research that men and women are not basically different in their sexual needs or functioning, or in their need for closeness and warmth, for pleasure and acceptance, the old roles still come into play—the man is active, the initiator, the conqueror; the woman is passive, the responder, the conquered.

Gail, a disillusioned thirty-seven-year-old divorced woman, reflects on what is happening: "It's still all performance for the man. They may like something different, like doing it on the kitchen floor instead of in bed, but that's all they know. And that's the tragedy. He resents the fact that she might be really turned on. He still wants it to be the struggle where she says, 'No, no, no.' And then when they're faced by women who want it? By women who know it will give them pleasure and who are willing to go after that pleasure? They can't handle it. What happens is most guys get a soft-on from this. So as a woman you get a choice: Either the old playacting and he's doing the same old thing, getting his strokes in the same old way, or you kind of do your own thing, all alone, even in bed with him. And either way, there's pain. I can't go back to the act anymore, there is no return to innocence."

As Dr. Yael Danieli, a psychologist, observed, "I've found that a lot of men take their woman's 'liberation' as a license to become passive. 'If you want to be liberated,' he says to her, 'you become the man. So in bed, I'll lie down and you will be the one who makes love to me.' He makes that decision and there is a lot of resentment. The result? Impotence. And the woman is resentful, too, for she feels cheated on both counts."

The woman is urged to change, does change, and in so doing runs counter to all the old role prescriptions for sexual behavior. She blames the man often for his failure to change along with her; he blames her for stepping too far beyond the recognized roles and asking too much of him. *The Hite Report* shows us only too clearly the anguish of women and the widespread misunderstanding about the nature of female sexuality. Psychologists tell us about the anguish of men, the impotence, the doubts and fears. And no one can offer a clear-cut solution.

A sex counselor related the following problem: "A woman and her husband showed up for counseling. She had been trying to make a lot of changes in herself and to grow. Her husband, a music teacher, was quiet and didn't seem to meet a lot of the new standards she had in mind. The more she got into being very active, outspoken, and successful at some of the new things she was trying, the worse it got. She became very heavy, laying trips on him, and he was not strong enough to counteract it.

"Sex had always been good before, so there was not a question of the problems being functional. But now they couldn't make it anymore, so they came in for the problem of sexual dysfunction. As they began working out some of the things, it became clear the problem wasn't sex. Although she was clearly delighted at being freed from the classic female social role, she was still demanding that he stay in the old masculine one. When they both realized that he wanted to change, too, and had changed, things straightened out, and sex was fine again. So the change in their relationship wasn't any great big deal they learned about sex, it was simply a question of getting them out of their stereotypical roles— together."

The counselor went on to say, "I know we can pull out sex and discuss it separately from everything else, yes; but the changes are not around sex alone. It's clearly around the role changes, and sex is a part of that. It's part of the whole issue of changing roles, which I think, by the way, is going to work out for the better."

The woman, too, shares some of the burden, some of the blame, for today's sexual dissatisfactions. She wants changes, and he may too, but if the changeover is to work, both must take into account their total conditioning as men and women. In one way, the sexual revolution and the changes in roles have pointed out and exaggerated the contrasts between men and women. Women, for all their emergence into liberation, still retain their conditioning to play a passive and expressive role. And men are still subject to their conditioning to play the macho role, conditioning that is still supported today by all the myths of prowess and the quest for genital sex. What would help is for each to have a share of the other's admirable qualities: the giving and receiving of warmth and closeness and tenderness that women have always associated with sex, the confidence, strength, the abandon and physicalness that men more readily show. Sex together could be enjoyed as a total experience, where the affection that surrounds the physical union is as important as the genital experience itself. Certainly men and women today both need patience with and great empathy for each other.

Looking at the problems people are having with sex, however, widespread as they are, cannot give us the total picture of what's happening with sex in marriage. There are a lot of people with good common sense who are not hyped up by the media, who do not try to live up to and beyond the new demands. One seldom hears from couples who are satisfied and working it all out. Good news is not news. Many are

having better sex and more sex than ever. But sexual
satisfaction is not sensational, it does not make good
copy. Such couples seldom feel moved to write about
their quiet delight as much as a dissatisfied person
is moved to write about his or her anguish.

Kevin, a handsome, dark-haired, blue-eyed Irish-
man, says none of his friends are uptight about sex.
"They're open about sex, a lot of people talk about it
openly, but not to the point of saying my husband's
great in the sack or what a great piece of ass my wife
is. They feel that's nobody's business but their own.
They talk about sex—people do—but it's not their
main topic of conversation, nobody's preoccupied
with it. And I think men are just as interested in the
closeness of marriage as they are in the sex that goes
along with it. They're really interested in their families like I am; they have good relationships with their
wives. I think the warmth means a lot to them, I
think the family does. And the guys I've known for
years, since we were high school kids, who haven't
gotten married yet, that's what they're looking for—
someone to love, someone to love them, not just somebody to get into bed with."

On another level, that same attitude is expressed
by Carl, a well-educated man in his late forties who
lives in California. "Oh, hell," he says, "you have to
keep your head in this crazy whirl." Carl is a European, witty and charming, and has been married for
fifteen years to a woman he met in New York. Selma
is twelve years his junior, and their relationship has
gone through all the permutations, from old-line traditional, through arguments about role changes, to a
new kind of accommodation to their goals as individuals and as a couple. Carl says, "I'm so tired of
hearing about sex, money, and roles being the end-all
of people's relationships. On these levels you certainly find the figures to support a general malaise.
But if you assume that neither sex nor money nor

even marriage is a god, but only symbols for a relationship, you see something else going on. You can cater to the statistical view, looking at it very cynically and superficially, like pop culture writers do, and you can look at the statistics that support men losing their erections because women are too aggressive, and you will find support for this. But so many people I know, ourselves included, live on so many different levels and have so many different approaches that they are simply not adapting to what the media say, and what the peer-group pressures say they should adapt to. There's always more between wife and husband in a relationship than statistics; what they are creating and developing, this something else between them, has nothing to do with statistics.

"When I first came to this country twenty years ago, to satisfy a woman was a totally unknown thing. I asked a friend at that time if he satisfied his wife. Just the question itself was shocking to him. His attitude was, 'Who, me? Why should I?' But I wanted to satisfy my woman, and he thought I was extreme and 'European.' But that has all changed. It is an accepted fact today that you satisfy the woman."

In another way, the sexual revolution, despite its hazards, has been enlightening, especially in the area of marriage. We have learned that all the technical proficiency in the world cannot take the place of caring and trust between two people—those qualities so essential to experiencing the fullness of sexual response. We are more aware than ever that there is a direct connection between good, continuing sex and the basic components of a good marital relationship. Sex did need to be demythologized and put into its proper place in our lives—not as a force that controls us, but as something we can use for our benefit, for the fullest expression of our love for each other, as well as for the casual delight we take in each other.

We needed the extreme, perhaps, to find the balance —the realistic place for sex in our lives. I think that more and more people are finding that balance, quietly and without fanfare.

Roberta, a twenty-year-old college student, is characteristic of those who have a new perspective on sex and man–woman relationships. "I wouldn't go into marriage or a relationship with the idea that sex was going to remain as terrific as it was before. Sex becomes more fulfilling and more understanding in a realistic way when you live together. It just becomes less dramatized in your mind. It's not more terrific, but it gets better because there is a commitment and a concern for each other that we are sure of. You feel secure in it.

"When I marry, I would hope it would continue to grow that way, as long as the relationship continues to grow. If the relationship doesn't continue to grow, then the sexual part won't either. I think sex has a lot to do with a marriage being good, but the marriage isn't necessarily good because the sex is good. When you've got your marriage together, then your sex life will be, too."

The relationship we have in marriage and how we feel about ourselves and our partners enormously influences the way we relate sexually. Good sex therapy and counseling is based on that premise, and all the changes of the last decade or so should make us more aware of its significance.

Jim sees some positive aspects of the sexual revolution. He and his wife of seven years have gotten it together in their relationship despite the media, but he says, "In the last ten years, there's been so much on sexuality, so many different movements, gay, bisexual, straight, it makes people examine themselves. Am I missing something? Do I have certain impulses that I never recognized? It not only makes you more tolerant, but it also makes you really try to get more in touch with yourself, to make you know what you really need and want, rather than changing your style per se. It just makes you think a little more."

Some people do, perhaps, need more stimulus than others, like Barry who was quoted earlier as saying he needed a frequent change of sex partners. But even this kind of excitation can pall after a while, whereas pleasure in sharing sexuality, in a close relationship over time, can be constant. Too great an emphasis on the genital aspects of sex distorts our understanding and contributes to the confusion between the sensation of the moment, and that pleasure that can continue to grow throughout a relationship.

After ten years of marriage, Christine reflects, "What is happening, it seems to me, is that sex is dissociated from the rest of living. The notion we get through the literature and media is that sex is an entity in itself. Sex is supposed to be a total turn-on, all the time. Maybe it is possible for those who concentrate on sex exclusively, like one friend of ours who joined us at dinner the other night with his girl friend. All they did all evening was talk about the exercises they did to be in good sexual shape. It was sort of amusing. She wore a red dress, rather open and crossed at the bosom, and he kept tucking his hand into her dress. They couldn't talk about anything else; they were constantly in the process of preparing for sex, all day long. Maybe for them it *is* a total turn-on, but it seems to take a lot of concentration.

"When sex becomes an entity unto itself, it can't be as reflective as it is of moods and seasons in our lives. It just seems to be self-evident when you live it that it really is. But you're bucking the popular culture which says, 'If you're not sexually satisfied, do something about it, substitute a new partner, have better sex, go the sex therapy route, read manuals, get turned on.' It's always getting 'turned on,' and who says anything about the turned-off times which exist for everybody? For me, marriage gives you that sense that there is time for it all to work out, the vicissitudes of mood, or whatever."

Spontaneity cannot be programed, for all the last-ditch attempts at it by Total Women greeting their husbands at the door in Saran Wrap and nudie cowgirl costumes. The seasonality of sex, the turned-off and turned-on times, cannot be foreseen and planned for ahead of time. Of course, we all need a surprise now and then, a new number to play. But every night? What happens when she runs out of costumes? I can't help imagining a scenario where the Total Husband, after weeks of throwing down his briefcase at the door each night and chasing her around the table, finally comes home one night, throws down his briefcase, and says, "For Chrissake, tonight, for once, all I want is a martini and a newspaper." Spontaneity comes from a joyful impulse in a climate where you are free to be yourself, without artifice or pretense.

Even the Total (and Fascinating) Woman was a phenomenon of the sexual revolution, a backlash against our real gains in equality, combined with new freedoms in sex. But there is some evidence that the rush of experimentation and exploration is subsiding, losing its ability to titillate, now that people have seen it all. A young woman of twenty-three, who works for an advertising agency, said that the changed sexual climate made her think she could do it all—and she is echoing the thoughts of many men as well. "It happened that way for me. As a result of the sexual revolution, women had the attitude that 'OK, I can do it all. I can go into a bar and meet somebody and we can go home and have this shortcut to instant intimacy, and everything is going to be fine.' What I found was that nine times out of ten, when you woke up you didn't want to look at that person. You know, not even want to know him. And when he opened his mouth, you knew for certain you had nothing else in common at all." At least she can be honest about it, instead of presenting the façade of such total liberation that sex is reduced to a handshake.

The sexual revolution helped us to explore and understand our sexual selves, but having the lid taken off sex has been a tempering experience. Sure, we were inhibited before the revolution, puritanical, repressed, hypocritical. Then the circus came to town, and everyone ran wild through the fairgrounds like kids let out of school. And it was all for free, it was liberation. Now that the carrousel is slowing down, and everyone has had just a little bit too much cotton candy, there is a lot of reassessment going on. Our roles and our attitudes have been changed by it, but we have now a clearer view of what sex and sexuality are. It is a most important part of our lives, but it is still only a part. Only one ring of the circus.

15

Sexual Fidelity

With all the changes in the sexual area that married couples are dealing with, what has happened to sexual fidelity? Has the idea of sexual freedom and the general loosening of our sexual mores changed the basic premise of sexual exclusivity in marriage? With women's new freedoms, what has happened to the double standard?

We have seen that sexual fidelity is considered a responsibility of marriage. We have seen that young women are taking a second look at the new freedom in sex that is available. But what are the realities? It has always been more acceptable for the man to have extramarital sex. Even mothers and mothers-in-law would tell a resentful wife, "But you have to expect this, dear. You know men. They always do this. Forget it, he'll come back to you." Whether the double standard was justified as his playful boyishness, a biological necessity, or a prerogative of male dominance made little difference. It happened, and it hurt, even when the little woman waited at home to forgive him.

We may believe, and from good evidence, that the double standard is still operating in our society: For the most part, men still have more opportunity and perhaps more desire and tacit permission to play around than women. But with women's greater opportunities for economic independence, for education and mobility, with a more permissive sexual climate and effective contraception, the balance in the fidelity equation in marriage has shifted. If he can do it, now so can she, at least in theory.

Before we examine what the new balance might mean for marriage, let's set the scene with one man's indignant protest against a too sweeping generalization about sexual fidelity or lack of it. During a group interview, I asked the men how they felt about the single standard, about women's sexual freedom, the fact that now women have more opportunity to do the same as the men.

"Hey, what about us good guys who have always been around?" asked this man with considerable logic and some heat. "So what's new with women playing around? We've always been loyal and gone off to work and the whole shot, and come home. And what did we find? There's the wife fooling around with the milkman. That's not so new. What about us good guys who never fooled around? Really, there's an awful lot of good guys in this country."

However you may interpret his statement, the fact remains that there are many men and women who do not have extramarital sex. And it is often forgotten in looking at the percentages of those who do, that many are one-time flings only.

Nevertheless, when all the statistics are in, we can't deny that the woman now holds as many chips as the man in the power game, a new bargaining position in the game of marital fidelity. And the way it seems to have turned out is that the new balance of power has reinforced sexual fidelity, not because of coercion, which has never worked anyway, but because of a reevaluation of what sexual fidelity means to two people in a marriage.

A young woman in her early thirties expresses the change this way: "The real difference today is that a woman has a legitimate right to be angry if her husband cheats. She doesn't have to take it anymore. Women have taken this crap all along. She was the one who had to be flexible before, and to adapt if her husband played around. Now she doesn't have to be meek and understanding anymore because she has a lot of options open to her. If she has a job, she can walk out, or she can find other people, too, or she can demand a showdown. It's not so much an equal decision *not* to cheat, or even for *both* to have extramarital affairs, as it is a willingness to have it out in the open."

Rather than taking sexual fidelity—or infidelity—for granted, couples are now more open with each other in examining the meaning of fidelity in their lives, its values to them, and their feelings about it.

A man's viewpoint of what has happened is expressed by Dave, an advertising executive now in his second marriage. "Historically men have always cheated, both publicly and privately. Of course, women have done it privately too. But now, for the first time, we are articulating fidelity and meaning it. Men for the first time are calling themselves up short and wondering, as I do, if their wives have the same feelings.

"I think women have always been able to deal with fidelity within a good marriage, but now, for the first time, men are having to deal with it too. Everyone gives up something in marriage, some kind of freedom to act. Women are giving up a lot of things in marriage, true, but belief in fidelity is not one of them. It's easier for her to be faithful. But men now are giving up a lot more, because they've always had the idea that they *could* play around. Even if they felt guilty, and I have in the past, they still felt it was their prerogative, or natural right, or whatever you want to call it. Today I don't feel that way at all. Oh sure, I still have the same old fantasies, but that is all they are, and I prefer it this way."

Although one could, of course, dispute Dave's contention that it is easier for women to be faithful, the more we hear and the more we learn, the more we confirm what we long ago knew: It is easier for both men and women to be faithful when there is love and understanding and respect in their marriages.

But what Dave *is* reflecting is a change in the attitude of men toward fidelity. In a recent Gallup poll, only one man out of four said he still believed in the double standard. Three out of four endorsed the same sexual rights and restraints for men and women alike. "The great majority think that men and women should have the same sexual rights and be bound by the same restraints. This turnabout is truly revolutionary," the study found.

I don't think this change came about because of any magnanimity on the part of men, or their sudden assumption that now, today, they had to start being faithful in marriage. I think it has come about for several reasons, not the least of which is the contemporary belief that we, as individuals, benefit more from our own control of certain aspects of our lives, rather than having them controlled by some outside agent. The ideal of equality for men and women has permeated every aspect of our relationships, and has become in turn an affirmation that sexual fidelity is to our advantage. Sexual fidelity as a positive and personal choice will always be more valuable than when we are coerced into it.

Another reason for the change is that people have had to cope with new freedoms and face realities in a way they never had to before. The freeing up of sex in other areas of our lives was bound to affect marriage and test the basic tenets of sexual exclusivity.

Sexual fidelity has always been one of the basic premises of marriage, whether or not it was carried out in practice. And for many good reasons. Apart from the ideal of two people who love each other sharing and reserving this most intimate aspect of self for each other, there were practical reasons. In the past, when effective contraception was not available, having exclusive sex with a wife assured a husband that he was father to the child, and assured the child of legitimacy and inheritance. Marriage also used to be the only legitimate way to have sex. Few other societies in the world have had such general prohibitions on any sex outside marriage, premaritally or otherwise. Besides this, marital sex was an obligation by law—a man actually owned the right to his wife's sexual services, and in a much more direct and enforceable way than she "owned" his sexual services. Today, few people think they own the sexual services of another. Our bodies and their functions belong to each of us as an inalienable right, and are given or denied according to our own wishes, not as another's possession to be used at will.

Commenting on this, Dr. Robert Seidenberg, a psychiatrist and author, has written, "Autonomous persons cannot be chattels; the conjugal contract cannot include ownership of bodies or 'free access.' Similarly, a person's worthiness must be loosened from his sexual behavior. To consider a person moral solely on the basis of one's sexual impeccability cheapens virtue.

"Under the guise of the expectation of sexual fidelity is the covert demand for possession of the body and soul of the other. To insure this 'fidelity,' liberties and human rights which normally would prevail in society are abrogated. Demands for sexual fidelity, a generally accepted accompaniment of love and devotion, have too often taken on the force of total ownership of the mate."

Finally, sex between two people is a symbol of closeness, a gift to each other, a symbol of the love and loyalty they share. There is a deep association between sex as a physical act of closeness and our feelings of attachment and affection. As infants we are held and caressed, soothed and cuddled by our parents, and thus learn to associate physical closeness with love and security, especially in our culture where the child from earliest infancy is usually cared for by only one or two adults. Given this and our internalization of traditional expectations for sex with only one person, sexual fidelity is not just a vow in marriage or a moral or religious belief, but a need associated with our deepest emotions and our quest for emotional security.

This is one reason why, once we have promised and given our trust to another person in an area so closely associated with our feelings of security and dependence, the breaking of the pledge of sexual fidelity seems like an abandonment and arouses feelings of jealousy and insecurity. Even when sexual nonexclusivity is agreed on between partners, the same feelings often occur. Resentment, a feeling of rejection, anger, and insecurity follow, sometimes as strongly as they do when a clandestine affair is discovered or revealed.

Of course, people differ in their reactions to extramarital sex or these agreed upon outside sexual relationships. Some people, for a variety of reasons, are able to accept or tolerate their more or less secret extramarital sex and affairs; and some couples manage permissive sexual relationships with others without difficulty, but these couples are very rare. George and I have found very few in our research for whom this is a long-term viable life-style. These kinds of reactions may be due to personality differences or the quality of the relationship; but basically, for most people, a partner's infidelity elicits deep and upsetting emotions. The assurance of sexual fidelity is still an important and necessary attribute of most marriages and infidelity an extremely threatening situation. Some people, well aware that it might happen, say, "I know it's a possibility, but I don't want to hear about it. I don't want to know." Many individuals, for their own good reasons, are not prepared to deal with or cope with revealing their own or their partner's affairs.

Others, like Martin, are more philosophical. With Suzanne often working late, and often at her dinner meetings and social events he has no interest in attending, he says, "I've had guys say to me, 'Aren't you worried that Suzanne's going to get involved sexually while she's out working with all these men?' And my answer is always the same: I can't eat my guts out about it; it's just part of life. If Suzanne gets involved, just don't tell me about it. It's a possibility, sure, but I could get involved, too. She could get involved even if she were home and not working. I just can't worry about it. I guess in marriage, you have to feel that the other person cares enough about you that they will not do anything to hurt you."

With the changed sexual climate and people's personal attitudes toward these changes, there is some relaxation in the expectation for sexual exclusivity throughout the marriage. The isolated incident can be taken in stride by many couples in marriage today, as it probably has been in the past. A woman who has been married a long time and whose husband frequently travels, says, "Bob and I have been to hell and back in all these years together and we have a great marriage. I love him and he loves me, but never did I expect perfection. I know when he is gone, he will do what he wants. I don't attempt to dictate to him, I just say, 'Don't bring back any exotic diseases.'" In her case, and many others, it is the larger fidelity, the overall loyalty to each other and the unit, that is held more important. Sex, after all, is only one aspect of fidelity. It is not the single physical act that pains us, it is the loss of emotional security and the feeling of primariness that is most threatening.

Of course, deprivations in other areas of our life also affect our feelings about sex and fidelity. Sexual fidelity can't be isolated from the total context of life. As Dr. Seidenberg said, "Few of us now have 'nervous systems' strong enough to withstand the total sexual freedom of our mates. However, we should strive to worry more about fidelity in other areas of our living. We might more profitably be concerned with *fidelity* in our work, and with our ideals in the conduct of our public as well as personal affairs. This, in short, means being faithful to one's own identity, that is, being what you are supposed to be and doing what you are supposed to do. This writer suspects that the morbid and obsessive preoccupation with the faithfulness of the other represents a compensatory projection of the corrosion of one's own integrity— the doubts that exist about one's own real worthiness in areas other than sexual.

"Sexual fidelity must be kept in perspective; it is not the ultimate virtue, nor does it make a person moral. Fidelity to a mate, a friend, or a client encompasses a sincere concern for his fate and a respect for his human rights. One can be sexually faithful to a mate and deceive him or her in a myriad of ways both subtler and more vital."

"I think I would be being unfaithful to my husband," said a young wife, "if I badmouthed him to a man I was attracted to or even if I put him down in front of his friends. I know he would never do this to me, and that's the kind of loyalty that's very important to me."

However much we are aware—or unaware—of the subtleties of loyalty and fidelity, the fact is that most people subscribe to and need sexual fidelity in their marriages. Few people can build the necessary trust, the needed belief and assurance in each other, the sense of loyalty necessary to protect their new and developing relationship without many kinds of exclusivity, including sexual. For most people, sexual fidelity is a part of the larger emotional loyalty they share as a central premise in being married—and for most, it continues so throughout their marriage.

But like most good things we aspire to in life, sexual fidelity is an ideal. And ideals do not always take into account the realities of life. There are many reasons why people do not or cannot live up to the pledge of sexual fidelity. The catalog is endless: boredom, curiosity, frustration, anxiety, hypocrisy, innovation, a need to restore self-esteem, lack of intimacy, the desire for something more, and the one added by the sexual revolution, sexual freedom. Today, we think more about freedom in sex, and more about sex in general. While we may have no intention of having sex with someone outside our marriage, permissively or otherwise, we have come to terms with the possibility of being physically or emotionally attracted to someone else.

Maryanne, who is newly married, mentions the classic situation of attraction and how she dealt with it. "There is a guy at work who is devastatingly attractive," she says. "If I were single, he would be someone I would want to have an affair with, and I know the feeling is mutual. Once there, for a moment,

I was really tempted, and then decided, no. If I did succumb, there would be that loss of innocence. Once it's done, it's like you put your finger in the cake, and it's not going to look the same anymore, or feel the same either. I realized that I'd be attractive to a lot of people and be attracted to them, but I'm very attracted to my husband and very much in love with him. Who needs to satisfy something that could be only sexual? My relationship with my husband is sexual, but it's much more than that. It's affection; it's love."

Maryanne made the decision for herself. Other couples, like Sara and Dennis, who have talked about this kind of situation, find they don't always know how they really feel about it. "I think sexual fidelity in marriage is expected," Sara says, "but still we talked about it a lot, maybe more than was necessary. Before we were married, he used to say, 'I want you to feel perfectly free to do anything.' Even after we were married, we talked about it.

"But then I found that although he said it, he didn't really mean it. Do you know how I found out? A close friend of ours is a high school teacher and has been married just a year. I told him about her fling with one of her students, and you know what he said? 'But she's married!' I couldn't believe it. He didn't say, 'My God, she slept with a student?' but 'Why was she sleeping with someone else after being married?' So you see, in an offhand way, I discovered how he really felt about fidelity for all his talking about hypothetical situations and wanting me to feel free."

Sara and Dennis were paying lip service to the new liberation without carefully examining what their reactions might be. Other couples, like Chuck and Amy, do discuss the issue ahead of time. Their marriage is a practical, realistic, and loving one, neither imbued with the old romanticism nor overweighed with new and complex ideals.

Chuck: We really have reached the point where we can deal with having sexual relationships with other people. Not that we need it, but intellectually, I've always said that I don't think there is anything wrong with it. On an emotional basis, though, I would probably have a great deal of difficulty with it. I'm probably much more jealous and possessive than I realize. I know I would be terribly hurt if Amy came home one night and said she'd gone to bed with so-and-so. She did it once when we were living together.

Amy: And I felt awfully guilty, terribly guilty. But now we are married.

Chuck: If she had a sexual relationship now, I don't think I'd want to know too many of the details, let's put it that way. But I think I would want to know. If she had one, she would probably feel guilty and would tell me, but the fact that she came back would be reassuring. I would be shocked and then I would be hurt, but I think I could live with it and vice versa.

Amy: Well, not for me. I always say it would be hard for me as a widow after I kill him. If he went with another woman, I would kill him. On an intellectual level, I figure there's nothing wrong with it and it doesn't mean anything. It's like going to dinner with somebody else, which certainly doesn't disturb me. It doesn't make my dinner any less well prepared. But it's a risky kind of thing.

Chuck: Yeah. What if you get emotionally involved with the other person?

Amy: That's the point. It's too risky. We feel no need to have a sexual relationship with somebody else at this point. Maybe sometime later I could benefit from it. But I wonder.

Chuck: I think it would have to change our relationship, dilute it somehow.

Amy: Right now, I feel fidelity is really important in our marriage.

Chuck: Not only for sex, but just fidelity in general. In its broadest meaning, it's part of the whole thing of caring.

By discussing the possibility of extramarital sex, Chuck and Amy found that the reevaluation comes not only on an intellectual level but on an emotional one as well—and it is this awareness that is most important. They seem to vacillate, but they are really exploring their feelings and considering the impact such choices might have on their marriage—and they are reaffirming that sexual fidelity, at this point at least, is an essential component in their relationship.

It has often been assumed that an affair or sexual encounter outside the marriage, or even the desire, is an indication of something "wrong" with the marriage. But this is a very narrow view of the complex issue of infidelity and the part sex plays in our lives. What is meant by "wrong"? Something may be wrong with the marriage today and it may clear up tomorrow and in between there might be a single incidence of sexual infidelity. Most marriages have problems at one time or another, and extramarital sex is only one outlet, among many others, for the distress caused by these problems. And it seems likely that sudden infidelities in long-standing, comparatively happy marriages may have more to do with an individual's personal problems than with any problems in the marriage. It is difficult, though, for a husband or wife to see it in this detached way. The private hurt overshadows the impartial observation. Even understanding why it may be happening doesn't lessen the pain and resentment. The conditions that may lead to a lapse in sexual fidelity can come from a temporary malaise, a mid-life crisis, from job concerns, from basic personality differences, a difference in sexual desire, from retaliation, from rough and out-of-synch periods, from any number of troubles. Or it may occur for reasons that have nothing to do with distress at all: curiosity, physical attraction, or seduction. And when one or the other does transgress, what do you do? There is no easy answer or blanket rule for the responsibility we each must take for our own actions, for telling or not telling, or for judging the importance this situation has in our own individual marriage.

Other societies have always been a bit more broadminded about outside sexual liaisons; though the family was always held in esteem and kept together. I'm not advocating that we duplicate their sexual standards (or their chauvinistic attitude toward women), but I do think we should recognize that many of our problems in marriage have to do with our American attitude toward sex—on the one hand it is dirty; on the other, divine, never a natural, earthy, sensuous part of life. This attitude is only beginning to change. Here in our society, we have a lot of sexually deprived people, not only because of our righteous attitudes about sex (despite the revolution), but also because of our advertising, which pushes the young, the beautiful, the superficially attractive. Sexy means firm breasts, slim hips, and blond hair, and perhaps twenty-two as a maximum desirable age. Sexy means big muscles, flat stomach, tight blue jeans, a mustache, give or take a decade. No one mentions the full and profound sexual feelings couples still have after long years together. Advertisers don't encourage us to recognize real sexuality— that integral sexual identity people have that comes through in the way they talk, move, touch, taste, feel —no matter how much they weigh, how old they are, what color hair they have. Unfortunately, a lot of people don't feel good about themselves, or a real-life partner, when the ideal is that glossy centerfold. And if you don't have all of what you're told it takes, well, you're simply not in the running.

Our sexual egos *are* delicate, and should be

guarded carefully. But no one is perfect, not everyone has an ideal marriage, not all of us have the
strength to be saints, not all of us have mates who
make sexual fidelity inviting. No matter how strongly
we subscribe to the moral and practical values of
sexual fidelity, the fact is that not all marriages are
made in heaven, not all mates are good matches, not
all mates feel good about themselves or their partners all of the time, not all partners are prepared to
handle problems, to relate fully and openly in trust
and caring. And when push comes to shove, not all
of us can keep our haloes straight.

16

Making It Last

Making our marriages last is harder now than ever before. When I talk to men and women about marriage, I am sometimes uplifted about its chances, and sometimes discouraged. Some marriages are clearly not going to last; others, you can't tell. Some, of course, are making it; there are working, happy marriages all around us, couples successfully creating new balances, finding purpose and deep satisfaction in sharing their lives and coping with the realities at hand.

Each marriage, though, no matter how happy, is beset with problems of personality, survival, goals, the search for self, and the quest of our decade:

something more. Something more can be almost anything: success, money, peace, understanding, personal growth, even the very answer to human existence. Something more puts a lot of pressure on marriage. We have had a revolution of rising expectations. Times have changed, and it is not only in marriage but in every facet of our lives that we expect to have more satisfaction. We, today, ask an awful lot of each other in marriage. In addition to the responsibility and adjustment and compromise that the relationship has always entailed, we're now asking each other to make changes more quickly or to accommodate to our own changes.

Can we make our marriages last through all the changes in ourselves and in society? The new demands being made on marriage for change and self-fulfillment, indeed, the whole temper of our times, are making it more and more difficult. In this society where the demands are for instant gratification, instant intimacy, instant communication, instant everything, are we, I wonder, no longer aware of the flow and cycles of life, of our need for roots and continuity? Are we no longer able to accept the commitment of life together as growth? No longer able to last through the rough periods that inevitably come along in any marriage? The ever-increasing divorce rate seems to indicate we aren't. And yet, the desire for stability and security, the recognition of our needs for belonging and for being rooted in the constancy of another's affection are everywhere, running like a thread through everyone's story. Marriage can still provide all that—and something more. Is it that we give up too soon, too often, when it doesn't happen instantly?

"Marriage is a delicate balance," says Anne, whose marriage is making it. "Sometimes you will be off balance. Like sometimes at work you don't know what the hell you are doing and want to throw it all out. At other times you are getting such a kick out of it that you feel just super. Well, it's the same in marriage. Sometimes you have a mad desire for something and go on a binge, and then another time things are turned around. People don't want to recognize that marriage is that way, too. They think it is supposed to be level and balanced all the time, like a balanced diet. But some days you want ice cream, and some days you want potatoes."

I thought of my parents and the longevity of their marriage, then of my own, and of all the marriages and remarriages I've seen. I thought of my son and his wife and friends who had not made it, and of my other son, Brian. How would he fare in the future? Would any of them have the chance to experience the rhythms of life together with another person that George and I have? Or would the many long and good marriages that did last forever, like my parents', become rare and exotic exhibits in the future?

Certainly the pain of growth within a marriage is often no more painful than ending a relationship. We all go through some pain and confusion and even crisis as we pass from one phase of our life to another, whether married or not. If we want "more," we're not always going to get it, not in life, not easily. Something more from a relationship is only possible when we are willing to give something more to it. Our appetites have been whetted by all kinds of new expectations, which seem at odds with the durability of marriage, even threaten its basic premises. Everything new at the moment seems to work against the longevity of marriage—our temporary and disposable culture, our mobility, our changing values and ethics.

Yet in the face of all the new difficulties, I still have a positive feeling about the future of marriage. We are in a time of transition, testing the new, questioning the old, and forging new kinds of commitments. In the long run, when we have come through the changeover, I believe we will discover that marriage can run in tandem with our new needs. Marriage is flexible enough and sturdy enough to adjust to change and new expectations. Tempered by a new realism, men and women are still loving and learning, and working at it. Despite divorce and disillusionment, there are couples out there who are working out new patterns, learning that Rome wasn't built in a day, enjoying the benefits that marriage has always given —and something more. In the long run, I believe our new discoveries that each of us can be more and have more will not be at odds with the deep satisfactions and continuity that marriage can bring.

In the meantime, is it practical anymore to expect marriages to last sixty or seventy years? Can we be satisfied sharing our life with one other person through our longer life span, through all the phases of our adult life, through all the changes the outside world brings?

Though we marry believing it will be forever, believing it is the way for building into the future, forever is still an ideal. And considering everything that's happening, would it be more logical to expect that in the course of our lifetime we can have several kinds of relationships, marriage being only one of them? Should we perhaps seek relationships according to our differing needs in the varying phases of our life? As more and different life-styles are accepted, the idea of marriage as the best and only way to live is changing.

Why should marriage be for everyone? Though I believe that marriage for a long time with one other person is not only possible but can be a place for continued discovery, intimacy, and growth, I am also aware of the realities we face and the pulls that all the new options exert.

A variety of relationships in life, a variety of life-styles in marriage exist today, and all kinds of considerations enter into the question of their durability. People get married, raise a family, divorce, remarry, and start a second family. Some stay together for forty years and suddenly become single again. Young people live together for years, break up, live as singles, and finally choose someone to spend the rest of their life with. Think of the variety of arrangements possible today, combinations and permutations enough to need a computer to handle. Maybe all those varieties and arrangements would be possible if we could learn how to have good relationships while they last, then end them when necessary with a minimum of pain.

But we have to remember that we are dealing with human relationships, not input cards for a computer. It isn't so easy when human feelings are involved. We haven't learned how to drop out of and back into serious relationships without pain and a great sense of loss. Perhaps we never will, for the need to have a lasting relationship, for continuity and connections in our lives, still remains, even with all the changes around us. And I think it always will.

While people marry for love and a fulfillment of those needs, they also marry for all kinds of other reasons—for status, because of family pressure, because it is a fun thing to do, because of the party or the ceremony or the wedding presents, or because friends are getting married. And when marrying for such reasons, it is often to the wrong person. Marrying young and on the basis of physical attraction seldom helps anyone discover a premise for the marriage. Or, as a wife said, "I married John for his potential, not for the person he was, and it took years to work that out."

And then, some marriages may not last because the relationship simply wears itself out and can never be revitalized. When a couple makes an implicit contract to grow toward a specific goal, and when the growth cycle completes itself, there may be nothing left to the marriage. It may be time to move on separately. Only if they understand the contract they have made can they revise it and move on together to a new phase. All people differ in their tolerance to stress, in their flexibility, in their patience and understanding. They change and grow at different rates. When one partner changes, moves ahead more rapidly than the other, with differences becoming even greater, finding enough in common to make the marriage work may be all but impossible.

Divorce has become a release from intolerable pressures and can set us on another path of growth, can make us wiser, stronger. In fact divorce has become so common that it seems to be almost a necessary initiation into adult relationships. In second marriages, we have a second chance, an opportunity to correct some mistakes we made in the first one, to choose a more compatible partner, to know what our premises and goals in life are this time around. But there's no guarantee that second marriages are any more enduring than first marriages—more second marriages, in fact, end in divorce than first ones.

There's no guarantee at all about making any marriage last. Even living together first doesn't ensure lasting accord or happiness. And how do you explain the people who married by arrangement or on bare acquaintance who remain richly compatible throughout their lives? What we do know, however, is that today more than ever it depends on the two partners involved, the two selves who by choice and agreement share a purpose in their relationship, who are aware of the durability of the foundations of marriage.

My friend Kate claims that people shouldn't get married until they are over fifty. Kate is thirty-two, divorced, raising a child alone, and more than a little bitter. "Really, it's the people who are fifty who should get married. They are at a time of their life when they can say, 'I've played around, I've had it all, let's get married.' Neither of them can have children, and they're not going to hurt each other with other relationships. It's a more stable period of their lives, so they can settle down."

Extreme as her position is, it has some validity, and so do her reasons for expressing it. "Marriage for me at this point in my life is meaningless. It's a myth. It's a natural state for men who have always been adored and cared for, but it has changed for women. And children. Well, who's taking care of them now? When it busts up, the women take care of the children anyway." Kate, like many others, is naturally disillusioned. "Well, nothing is permanent," she commented. "For my generation, there are bigger and better things, like having many good relationships."

When you see the growing number of single and divorced people living alone, you wonder if it won't turn out that way, marrying at fifty. People are marrying later in life today. I married young, but that was in another time, another era. While early marriages often do turn out to be good ones, there are many reasons for waiting to get married until the mid or late twenties. There is too much life to be lived before we are ready for the commitment of marriage. We need time to know ourselves, to develop our skills of perception, to outgrow the distortions of youthful imagination. For all the acceleration of life today, it still takes us twenty-some years and more to get our feet on the ground, to know something of what we are about and where we want to go, to find an identity of our own.

A young man told me, "I've spent twenty years of my life in school, and when I graduate, I have a chance to do whatever I want to do, and getting married has got to be the last choice on my list."

Another young man in a group of students I spoke to gave a reason that sounded curiously like the way people used to talk in the old days of dowries and furniture paid for before the wedding: "You should establish yourself first, travel and establish yourself financially. You have to have finances to be able to be married and support somebody else or to enjoy one another. But now is the time to do what you've wanted to do, to go ahead and do it. You don't have any attachments. I can't see getting married until later on, closer to thirty."

Many single women said they wanted to establish their careers and get an education before they married. All good and justifiable reasons for waiting until later. A young woman, a university undergraduate, said, "I'd rather wait. I know a lot of people who feel that if they aren't married by twenty-one, half their life will be wasted. But I feel I've got a lot of time ahead of me. It's better if I learn to depend on myself, be my own person, do my own thing. I don't want to make a commitment to someone else not knowing who I am."

Waiting until you are older to marry is still no guarantee of success, of course, but the chances for understanding yourself and your partner are far better. When we are young, our relationships give us time to experiment, to understand our needs and how to mesh them with another's, and they are good and valuable experiences.

When we marry too young, still depending on the protection of a natural and early possessiveness, we tend to limit the discoveries of our selves, learning what our tolerances are, for instance, exploring the areas and dimensions of self into which we can expand. We need the advantage of knowing and relating to many other people, people other than our families and our first infatuations. The danger of marrying too young is not that our choices may be wrong, but that we ourselves are as yet unformed.

One of the young men in a class I spoke to said, "I was in a group of six guys and we were pretty close. They are all married and I'm the only one now who is single. They all said they wished they had waited two or three years longer before they married. They all married at twenty-one or twenty-two, just at the time I started to travel around the country, and they said they missed out on that. They wished they had waited, but all of them said they would have married the same girl."

I was amused to see certain things show up over and over in my interviews. The advantage of being able to travel turned up as often for the young and unmarried as the comfort of having clean laundry turned up for marrieds. Perhaps the freedom represented by travel is contrasted with some of the old illusion of marriage as a limiting, confining experience.

Another person I spoke with said, "Society puts a lot of pressure on people, but my personal opinion is that people should get married when they are twenty-five. Forever is a long time, and you figure that everybody lives until they're seventy, and that is forty-five years you are going to spend with someone. So I wouldn't do it. No way. Even at twenty-three or twenty-four. And especially at nineteen; you aren't mature enough to get married. It's too much of a commitment."

If marriage is the important intimate and profound relationship we know it to be, if it is as difficult yet rewarding as we have found it to be, it is not something to be taken lightly, to be entered into as a lark —especially when we have so many other living arrangements to choose from today. And while I know it might be better to wait until you have experienced something of life, have gotten an education, have tried life on your own and found out something about your place in the scheme of things before you marry, there are also some inherent snags built into that proposition, some undesirable consequences, too, perhaps inevitable ones. As you get older, you do become less resilient, less able to accommodate another person's ways. You become, in that very old and well-known phrase, "set in your ways." At least that's what we've always thought.

One father of nearly grown-up sons says, "I see a very important and basic difference in my kids in the fact that the expectation for getting married is

no longer what it used to be. A lot of kids don't think
in terms of getting married. They don't want to get
married, or at least they don't want to get married
early. I think there's a lot more trying out than we
would have ever dreamed of doing. I don't know
that the outcome can be predicted yet. My own
feeling is probably that it's a good idea. But I don't
know, for example, if my wife and I had met at this
point in our lives whether we would have gotten
married. There's an excitement that may be lost if
you put it off too long."

One of the developing patterns in American life
today is that a lot of people are staying single. Recent
figures show that since 1970, a startling 134 percent
more persons under the age of thirty-five are living
alone. Many are there because they want to be there
and prefer their single life-style. They never want to
marry. No one today could claim, as we did in the
old days, that marriage is best or even good for everyone. Sometimes, though, single people tend to
close themselves off, become too self-indulgent in
their aloneness and unable to adjust to others. A great
many singles, however, have made a responsible choice
to remain single and are creating full, satisfying, and
diversified life-styles, and making a rich life of a
complement of many different relationships. As a
woman friend of mine put it: "Why should I give up
the exciting tenderness of Paul, camping trips with
Bill, the protective fatherliness of Al, the romantic
pedestal Roger sets me on, or earthy fun and games
with Jack. They're all parts of my life, but I don't
want any one to the exclusion of all the others, all
the time. Living alone, I have my career and the
variety I want, pretty much when it suits me—and
with no one keeping tabs on me."

Variety is still the spice of life, and perhaps today's
options, and the self-fulfillment decade, have empha-
sized this. But as with any design for living, marriage

included, some things are left out. And I believe that there are certain discoveries that can be made, certain levels of growth reached, only when a person lives with another person over a span of time. We live in one way with our families as children and young people, and we live in quite another way with others as adults. It is away from our families, on our own, that we are able, through a close adult relationship, to gain a broad perspective of life, to temper our distortions and predilections, to become more compassionate, to grow in our capacity for giving to and receiving from others.

But perhaps the fear of marriage has permeated too deeply. And maybe that fear goes deeper than we want to admit, and makes it easier for us to avoid the risk of getting close to another. If we had more proponents for marriage, more concern for family and the benefits of bonding, more awareness of how marriage can change us, and more education in marriage, and family life, and parenting, we might have more courage to undertake the commitment of relationships.

If we do decide to marry, whether it is earlier or later, we should be aware of why. Making the marriage last depends on many other aspects of our relationship besides the foundations, the basic premises of marriage. We must be aware of the rhythm, the cycles of life and how they affect our lives together. We must expect tension and conflict to arise from time to time; it is through resolving our conflicts and understanding the dynamism of tension that we grow. The discoveries we make about each other in our different phases of life together can make life interesting and exciting.

We can make the marriage last by restoring the romance and ritual in our lives, not by indulging in sentimentality or an attempt to recapture the past, but with a deep understanding of the vital role they play in our relationships. Romance and ritual are our ways of touching once again the symbols of our connection with each other; it is a way of reestablishing our relationship, a soaring above the everyday to reaffirm our meaning to each other. As Jenny says, "Habit, routine, and ritual; they have different connotations. Habit is something regular, routine is kind of dull, but a ritual is something special. When we were dating, we used to make calls to each other from a certain phone booth. We still pass that corner a lot, and whenever we do, we always grab each other and kiss. This is our spot, our corner. I know that if I'm a ninety-year-old lady and I walk past that corner, it's going to be the same."

"I think," says Karen, "that there has to be a little bit of romance; I don't think it's dead for us. Not all this kissing and hugging, because that's phony in large doses. But you have your moments and your times and a certain warmth that you share. It's not the sort of romance you see in the movies, but if it were completely dead, I don't think I would be married."

Romance and ritual are things we seem to have lost in our contemporary world. They have been devalued, like our relationships. Yet ritual, in particular, has always been important as a confirmation of unity and shared values among people in groups, and it is more important than we realize for married people.

"There are people," says an older married woman, "who really set great store by their rituals, which sort of outline their history together. I personally feel that when you start out in marriage, you start out being greedy, maybe of love, maybe of something else, but as you continue to be married, you develop a friendship, and then you move into a family relationship, into a style of life and values, and each is a step along the road, a historical landmark. You don't exactly know where the expedition will take you, but you may savor the landmarks along the way."

Such shared rituals and ceremonies have an important function in our lives, and in marriage there are also those private and personal ones we create for ourselves in our relationship. "We have a ritual where the last ten minutes just before we go to sleep at night we talk," one woman says. "Our daily routines keep us apart, but this is our time for bringing it all together."

Although it may seem debatable today, children do play an important part in keeping marriages together and alive. Once we decide to take on the responsibility of a family, longevity in a marriage is most important. A man and a woman can begin and end the marriage when they choose, but what about the children? What do they have to say about it? There is evidence that the child and the family as a unit are the lowest on our list of public priorities. But public priorities notwithstanding, the family is the basic unit of society, and our most important institution. And there should be a major concern for keeping marriages healthy and intact during the period of child raising—no matter how urgent our journey to find the self.

In the case of unhappy marriages where there are already children, no one can say categorically whether or not they all should or should not be held together for the sake of the children or which choice will be less destructive to everyone involved. But for those not yet married, or who have not yet made the decision to have children, there should be serious consideration beforehand whether or not the marriage is likely to last through that period of child raising. There should be a concern for the quality of the marriage relationship that so surely determines the quality of the family life they will all make together. Even with divorce and remarriage, except in very unusual circumstances, the continuing relationship of each parent to the child is essential to the child's welfare.

Marriage is a place where we learn to give and to receive, and ultimately reaffirm our belief in the good and valuable in our lives. As a therapist said of his own marriage: "I see marriage as a reflection of our highest values; I think that is what love is. When you say to someone I love you and want to marry you, then that marriage presents a commitment to that value system. I think that when two people commit themselves to a relationship, they are saying a great deal, first about themselves, about who they are and what they think they deserve and what they want out of life and what the relationship does for them. And second, they are saying a great deal about their value system."

We create ourselves by the choices we make; we create our marriages and our value systems by the choices we make. And for all the changes in our lives today, many of the old values still remain, and the basis of marriage still reflects those values. For all the different premises couples can have for their marriages, marriage is still the commitment of two people through time, with connections to others, with a primary concern for each other's well-being, and with an understanding that no matter how much we redefine and change our responsibilities, responsibility is still an integral part of marriage.

In the outside world, we can achieve satisfaction from gaining status and admiration, wielding power, maneuvering people, or becoming president of a corporation. Marriage brings us a whole different set of satisfactions that we experience only within ourselves and in our relationship—the profound satisfactions of making life more orderly, more pleasant, more joyful, more spontaneous, warm, and loving for ourselves and another person; the satisfaction of being known and accepted for what we are. Marriage is our place for intimacy, for supporting each other in growth, for joining with someone to share a common purpose in life.

We are here to celebrate life together, and if we believe in the value of marriage and want to make it work, it can give us more of what we want and need than any other existing arrangement for living. If it is our choice, then it is worth making it last.

Notes and References

Chapter 1: Beginnings

p. 3: *Betty Friedan* . . . (*welcome prophet though she was*):
This reference, of course, is to Betty Friedan's trail-blazing
book *The Feminine Mystique* (New York: W. W. Norton &
Company, 1963).

Chapter 2: Change

p. 5: *Open Marriage: A New Lifestyle for Couples* by Nena
O'Neill and George O'Neill (New York: M. Evans and Co.,
1972; Avon Books, 1973). *Shifting Gears: Finding Security
in a Changing World* by Nena O'Neill and George O'Neill
(New York: M. Evans and Co., 1974; Avon Books, 1975).

Chapter 3: Marriage Makes a Family

p. 19: *Living together:* Eleanor D. Macklin's continuing research on this topic and her newsletter are significant and invaluable contributions to our understanding of these arrangements. *The Cohabitation Research Newsletter* is compiled and edited by Dr. Eleanor D. Macklin, Dept. of Psychology, State University College, Oswego, N.Y. 13126, and distributed under the auspices of the Groves Conference on Marriage and the Family.

p. 23: This reference to the *almost mystical bond* appears in Robert Briffault and Bronislaw Malinowski's *Marriage: Past and Present,* edited, with an introduction, by M. F. Ashley Montagu (Boston: Porter Sargent, 1956), p. 69.

p. 26: *enduring, diffuse solidarity:* is from David Schneider's *American Kinship: A Cultural Account* (Englewood Cliffs, N.J.: Prentice-Hall, 1968), pp. 52–53.

pp. 26–27: *a separate and distinct entity from the "me" and "you":* An excellent, analytical description of the interactions and types of relationships between the "you," "me," and "us" has been made by Dr. Max Garfinkle in his paper, "Toward a Science of Couples," presented at the Annual Conference of the National Conference on Family Relations, in New York City, October, 1976. Helpful suggestions also appear in Dr. Gerald Walker Smith's *Couple Therapy* (New York: Macmillan Publishing Co., Inc., 1973).

Chapter 4: Golden Wedding

p. 36: Malinowski's quote is found in Briffault and Malinowski, op. cit. p. 83.

Chapter 5: House of Marriage

p. 39: Simone Weil's statement is in her book *The Need for Roots,* trans. Arthur Wills (New York: Harper & Row, 1952), p. 10.

Chapter 6: Marriage Makes a Place

p. 44: The book I have found most helpful in explaining the many aspects of intimacy is Murray S. Davis's *Intimate Relations* (New York: The Free Press, 1973).

p. 51: Dr. Yael Danieli is on the Faculty of the National Institute for the Psychotherapies and is a psychotherapist in private practice doing individual, family, and group work in New York City.

Chapter 8: Connections and Kinship

p. 73: Margaret Mead is quoted from her column in *Redbook* (May 1975).

Chapter 9: Time of Our Lives

p. 81: Dr. Lewis Wolberg is founder and trustee of the Postgraduate Center for Mental Health and clinical professor of psychiatry at New York University Medical School.

Chapter 10: Responsibility

pp. 88–89: The change from external coercion to internal cohesion in marriage was set forth in detail by Ernest Watson Burgess and Harvey J. Locke in *The Family: From Institution to Companionship* (New York: American Book Co., 1945).

p. 97: Martin Buber's quote is from his book *I and Thou*, trans. Ronald Gregor Smith (New York: Charles Scribner's Sons, 1950), p. 28.

Chapter 11: On the Road

pp. 111–12: *It wasn't so much marriage per se, but the prevailing kind of marriage:* Out of this insight grew our suggestion for more flexibility and change in marriage, a marriage that could incorporate equality and growth for both wife and husband. Fundamental to our concept of *Open Marriage* (op. cit.) is the belief that the individual can be and is a powerful force for institutional change. We have explored this in a paper entitled "Open Marriage: A Synergic Model," *The Family Coordinator* (Vol. 21, No. 4, Oct. 1972), pp. 403–409.

p. 112: *It is not an easy or a fair choice:* In an address at the Annual Meeting of the Grove Conference on Marriage and the Family in Dallas, Texas, in 1972, we suggested ways in which human service systems could change to accommodate and facilitate greater equality in marriage and shared parenthood. See our paper entitled "Open Marriage: Implications for Human Service Systems," *The Family Coordinator* (Vol. 22, No. 4, Oct. 1973), pp. 449–456.

Chapter 12: Men and Women

p. 116: Plato's *two halves* is a more complicated image than the part I have quoted and appears in *Dialogues of Plato* (New York: Pocket Books, 1950), pp. 188–193.

p. 117: The quotation is from Dr. Barry Certner's *Sex Roles and Mental Health: A Proposal for the Development of the Sex Roles Institute.* Copyright: Barry Certner (published and supported by a grant from the Psychiatric Institute Foundation of Washington, D.C., 1976), Chap. II, p. 26.

p. 122: *As a family therapist points out:* the quote is from Dr. Yael Danieli.

pp. 123–24: Dr. Rollo May's statement about myths was made in his address at the 84th Annual Convention of the American Psychological Association in Washington, D.C., 1976.

p. 126: *more than two million women earn more than their husbands:* An estimate of 2.3 million was made by Carolyn Shaw Bell from government statistics and reported in Marilyn Bender's article "Why Working Wives Feel Guilty," in *McCall's* (Aug. 1974), p. 40. An estimate of 1.8 million was made by Carl Rosenfeld of the government's Division of Special Labor Force Studies, and reported by Letty Cottin Pogrebin in her column "The Working Woman" in *Ladies' Home Journal* (Feb. 1976), p. 70.

p: 126: *Today women do not have to marry:* "In the group in which men and women traditionally marry (20–24), the percentage of women remaining single has risen from 28% in 1960 to 39% in 1974—an increase of one third." This may indicate either a later marriage age or a growing commitment to lifelong singleness: it is too early to say. These statements were made by Roxann A. Van Dusen and Eleanor Bernert Sheldon in "The Changing Status of American Women," *American Psychologist* (Feb. 1976), pp. 106–116.

p. 127: Dr. Estelle Ramey's statement was made at an address during a conference held December 1–3, 1976, in Washington, D.C., and appears on p. 18 of a report entitled *Proceedings of a Conference on Sex Roles and the Mental Health of Society,* prepared by Gabriel Heilig and Kirti Love-Heilig for the Sex Roles Institute, 2033 K Street, N.W., #202, Washington, D.C. 20006.

p. 128: *a different emotional language:* and following quote is from an article by Letty Cottin Pogrebin, "Can I Change Him?," *Ms.* (Jan. 1977).

Chapter 13: The Home Front

p. 145: Jeff Greenfield's article "What I Learned About Myself from My Three-Year-Old Daughter" appeared in *Glamour* (Sept. 1976). Carrie Carmichael, his wife, has written a book titled *Non-Sexist Child Raising* (Boston: Beacon Press, 1977).

Chapter 14: What's Happened to Sex in Marriage?

p. 154: *married couples in every age group are having more sex today:* see Jane Brody's article "Sexual Activity Found Increasing" in *The New York Times* (Oct. 8, 1974).

p. 161: Shere Hite's analysis of 3,000 responses to her questionnaire appears in *The Hite Report: A Nationwide Study of Female Sexuality* (New York: Macmillan Publishing Co., 1976).

p. 167: *The Total Woman* by Marabel Morgan (Old Tappan, N.J.: Fleming H. Revell Co., 1973). See Joyce Maynard's article "The Liberation of Total Woman" in *The New York Times Magazine* (Sept. 28, 1975) and reactions in "Letters," *The New York Times Magazine* (Oct. 19, 1975).

Chapter 15: Sexual Fidelity

p. 172: The quotation and information on change in men's attitudes toward the double standard are from Morton Hunt's report "Special: Today's Man, *Redbook*'s Exclusive Gallup Survey on the Emerging Male," in *Redbook* (Oct. 1976).

p. 173: *Few other societies in the world:* George Peter Murdock, writing in 1949 and drawing on his comparison of world societies, stated: "From available evidence, however, it seems unlikely that a general prohibition of sex relations outside marriage occurs in as many as five percent of the peoples of the earth." Premarital license, for instance, prevailed in 70 percent of his sample. *Social Structure* (New York: The Free Press, 1949), pp. 263–265.

p. 173: Robert Seidenberg is quoted from his book *Marriage Between Equals: Studies from Life and Literature* (New York: Anchor Press/Doubleday, 1973), p. 329.

p. 174: *Even when sexual nonexclusivity is agreed on between partners, the same feelings can occur:* I am saying this and have found it to be the case despite the widespread misinterpretations that were made of *Open Marriage* when it was published five years ago. In describing our model for an ideal marriage of equality, George and I devoted the book to suggesting how couples might build a relationship of trust, intimacy, and commitment through true sharing and caring. As an entirely optional consideration, and not as an integral part of our model for an open marriage, we opened up the topic of outside relationships. We suggested that fidelity could be seen in the light of the larger loyalty the partners had to each other and to their mutual growth, rather than as ownership of the mate or exclusivity. We suggested that some couples who had developed the necessary trust, open communication, and feeling of primariness in their marriage *might*, as individuals, have a supplementary relationship with another person that did include sex, agreed to mutually, openly, and honestly between them.

We presented that possibility idealistically but with a caveat concerning freedom, responsibility, and fidelity to their relationship. We thought that a couple who had already developed the kind of emotionally secure and strong primary relationship we spent the whole book describing would be able to deal with the issue of sex outside their marriage. Based on our research, we also felt that open and honest discussion of desires and fantasies would not only defuse desires and minimize jealousy, but also avoid undermining the primary relationship through cheating. We did not discuss the motivations, the logistics, the pitfalls, the benefits, or the emotional consequences of experimenting with sex in any other context or in any other kind of relationship outside the marriage.

We were thus surprised to see *open marriage* become a term, not for the new relationship of equality we had described, but for everything from a *sexually* open marriage to almost anything else. For some people it meant what we intended; for others it meant nonmarriage; but for the majority it meant whatever they imagined it to be. Like a Rorschach test, it mirrored the readers' perceptions, to say nothing of the perceptions of those who did *not* read it but thought they knew what it was all about. It was most often misinterpreted as open sex, and so became a convenient label for everything from a non-caring, do-your-own-thing relationship to an intellectual justification for what people had been doing sexually all along, or wished they were doing. There were, however, many sincere couples who did understand our intent and who believed in freedom and nonpossessiveness along with commitment. But those couples were not looking for justifications or guidelines. They had already been experimenting with open relationships.

For others, a try at having outside relationships was often a last-ditch attempt to save what seemed already a terminally ill marriage. When they couldn't agree on anything else, this was something they could agree on. But it could hardly be expected to work for two people who already had grave problems in their marriage. For yet others, it was a try at keeping up with the Joneses in liberation. Instead of listening to their own feelings, they listened to others and also found it didn't work; they had opened up their marriages in the area they could least afford to be open in. Still others, with good marriages, began from a position of principle about sexual freedom and found it to be an emotional minefield, filled with pain—and discovery. For them there were benefits, and growth. Most kinds of growth are painful, and this one, in an area that touches our fundamental feelings of security, turned out to be especially painful. As one man said, "We always put up this great front of liberation, because we were afraid to face how serious the problems were in our marriage. For us, the whole thing, painful as it was, was a revelation. It made us finally confront what our problems really were and how much we meant to each other."

Many returned once again to sexual exclusivity, to work out better the problems they had between themselves. Many of those returned with an agreement that, though the doors were always open, they were choosing not to walk through them. And that made them feel less bound and more joyful in their voluntary choice to be sexually exclusive.

These experiments with sexually open relationships, whether under the aegis of sexually open marriage or not, led to a reevaluation and redefinition of what was important and indispensable in the marriages of those involved. For all its applications, interpretations, and misinterpretations, sexually open marriage is still one possibility—but only, and then only rarely, in the context of a marriage fully open in every other respect. We never suggested it was for everybody, and I do not suggest it now. For most people, sexual exclusivity is still a fundamental premise in marriage and a symbol of their loyalty to each other.

p. 175: *These kinds of reactions may be due to personality differences:* There is some indication that those who do try sexually open arrangements may have a particular constellation of personality characteristics. In her sample of sixteen couples, Dr. Jacquelyn Knapp found that the majority fell into one of three categories: extroverted intuitive, introverted intuitive, and introverted feeling. She states: "While estimations place the number of intuitives in the general population at about 25 percent, they made up 88 percent of the sample. . . . If further research upholds the personality trends observed with this small sample, then certain types of people indeed might be attracted to SOM [sexually open marriage] and be able to manage such a complex life-style successfully." See "Sexually Open Marriage and Relationships: Issues and Prospects," by Jacquelyn J. Knapp and Robert N. Whitehurst, in *Marriage and Alternatives: Exploring Intimate Relationships* (Glenview, Ill.: Scott, Foresman and Co., 1977), pp. 147–160.

p. 175: *there is some relaxation in the expectation for sexual exclusivity throughout the marriage:* But not as much as we might think. In a 1973 National Opinion Research Poll of 1,491 adults, 70 percent said that extramarital relations were always wrong. An additional 15 percent said they were almost always wrong. However, the fact that the remaining 15 percent viewed extramarital sexual relations as "wrong only sometimes" or "not wrong at all" is, as the author of the report notes, an important, if minor, shift from our traditional norm. These data and analyses appear in David L. Weis's paper, "An Analysis of American Attitudes Toward Extramarital Sexual Relations: Survey Research Utilizing N.O.R.C. Data," delivered at the Annual Convention of the National Council on Family Relations, New York City, October 21, 1976.

p. 176: Robert Seidenberg's quote: op. cit., pp. 329–330.

Chapter 16: Making It Last

p. 192: *since 1970, a startling 134 percent more persons under the age of thirty-five are living alone:* for a discussion of the latest U.S. Bureau of the Census figures, see "Trend to Living Alone Brings Economic and Social Change," *The New York Times* (Mar. 30, 1977).

ABOUT THE AUTHOR

NENA O'NEILL is an anthropologist who has spent many years researching modern marriage. With her husband, George O'Neill, she is the co-author of *Open Marriage: A New Lifestyle for Couples,* and *Shifting Gears: Finding Security in a Changing World.*

ALL FOR THE FAMILY

Choose from this potpourri of titles for the information you need on the many facets of family living.

☐	12208	**THE FUTURE OF MARRIAGE** Jessie Bernard	$2.75
☐	12179	**LOVE AND SEX IN PLAIN LANGUAGE** Eric W. Johnson	$1.50
☐	12208	**THE PLEASURE BOND** Masters & Johnson	$2.50
☐	02814	**DARE TO DISCIPLINE** J. Dobson	$1.95
☐	02108	**A PARENT'S GUIDE TO CHILDREN'S READING** Nancy Larrick	$1.95
☐	11385	**P.E.T. IN ACTION** Thomas Gordon with J. Gordon Sands	$2.50
☐	12296	**THE FUTURE OF MARRIAGE** J. Bernard	$2.75
☐	10536	**THE BOYS AND GIRLS BOOK ABOUT DIVORCE** Richard A. Gardner	$1.50
☐	11378	**HOW TO GET IT TOGETHER WHEN YOUR PARENTS ARE COMING APART** Richards & Willis	$1.75
☐	11037	**WHO WILL RAISE THE CHILDREN?** James Levine	$1.95
☐	11776	**NAME YOUR BABY** Lareina Rule	$1.75
☐	11227	**YOU AND YOUR WEDDING** Winnifred Gray	$1.95
☐	11365	**OF WOMAN BORN: Motherhood as Experience and Institution** Adrienne Rich	$2.95

MS READ-a-thon—
a simple way
to start youngsters reading.

Boys and girls between 6 and 14 can join the MS READ-a-thon and help find a cure for Multiple Sclerosis by reading books. And they get two rewards — the enjoyment of reading, and the great feeling that comes from helping others.

Parents and educators: For complete information call your local MS chapter, or call toll-free (800) 243-6000. Or mail the coupon below.

Kids can help, too!

We Deliver!
And So Do These Bestsellers.

Bantam Book Catalog

Here's your up-to-the-minute listing of over 1,400 titles by your favorite authors.

This illustrated, large format catalog gives a description of each title. For your convenience, it is divided into categories in fiction and non-fiction——gothics, science fiction, westerns, mysteries, cookbooks, mysticism and occult, biographies, history, family living, health, psychology, art.

So don't delay——take advantage of this special opportunity to increase your reading pleasure.

Just send us your name and address and 50¢ (to help defray postage and handling costs).

BANTAM BOOKS, INC.
Dept. FC, 414 East Golf Road, Des Plaines, Ill. 60016

Mr./Mrs./Miss_____
                           (please print)

Address_____

City_____ State_____ Zip_____

Do you know someone who enjoys books? Just give us their names and addresses and we'll send them a catalog too!

Mr./Mrs./Miss_____

Address_____

City_____ State_____ Zip_____

Mr./Mrs./Miss_____

Address_____

City_____ State_____ Zip_____

FC—9/78